MATCHING CLIENTS AND SERVICES

SAGE HUMAN SERVICES GUIDES, VOLUME 21

SAGE HUMAN SERVICES GUIDES

a series of books edited by ARMAND LAUFFER and published in cooperation with the Continuing Education Program in the Human Services of the University of Michigan School of Social Work.

A **SAGE** HUMAN SERVICES GUIDE **21**

MATCHING CLIENTS AND SERVICES
Information and Referral

R. Mark MATHEWS
Stephen B. FAWCETT

Published in cooperation with the Continuing Education Program in the Human Services of the University of Michigan School of Social Work

SAGE PUBLICATIONS   Beverly Hills   London

For information address:

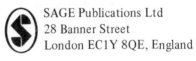

SAGE Publications, Inc.
275 South Beverly Drive
Beverly Hills, California 90212

SAGE Publications Ltd
28 Banner Street
London EC1Y 8QE, England

Printed in the United States of America

Library of Congress Cataloging in Publication Data

Mathews, R. Mark,
    Matching clients and services.

    (A Sage human services guide ; 21)
    "Published in cooperation with the Continuing Education Program
in the Human Services of the University of Michigan School of Social Work."
    Bibliography: p.
    1. Social service–Information services–United States. I. Fawcett,
Stephen B. II. University of Michigan. Continuing Education Programs in
the Human Services. III. Title. IV. Series: Sage human services guides ; v. 21)
HV41.M36   361'.007   81-4337
ISBN 0-8039-1619-1 (pbk.) AACR2

SECOND PRINTING, 1983

CONTENTS

A NOTE TO THE PROGRAM DEVELOPER

Providing information about community resources and service organizations is often the most basic service offered by volunteer programs, neighborhood service centers, and other social service agencies. Because the needs of multiproblem clients rarely match the offerings of a single agency, agency personnel need information about what services are available through other organizations within the community. The proliferation of service agencies and their specialized problem-solving capabilities add to the complexity of locating the most appropriate community resource for a particular client problem. Only after many years of experience and network building do the most experienced service-givers formulate their own informal social service directories. As a result, it is virtually impossible to efficiently share this accumulated knowledge with other potential helpers in the community.

A major goal of this book is to describe how you can develop a comprehensive information and referral system for your community. The social service directory described in this book is designed to be inexpensive and to be usable by both professional and nonprofessional staff of a variety of service organizations. Widespread adoption of this information and referral system in your community may well foster interagency coordination and, in turn, improve service delivery to clients. Part I of this book describes a method that we found to be useful in developing an information and referral directory, promoting interagency feedback, and training community service workers in the skills involved in providing a referral. Part II details a recommended method by which service-givers can provide referrals to other social service agencies.

The preparation of this book was made possible by the input, cooperation, and encouragement of a number of people. We are indebted to Ocoee Miller, Kay Fletcher, and Jim Olsen for countless discussions of community service delivery on which this information and referral system is based. Feedback on the components of the referral program was provided by the staff members at the Douglas County Council on Aging, ECKAN, and the Penn House Neighborhood Service Center. Jim Meyer and a number of other fieldwork students at the University of Kansas provided invaluable assistance in interviewing social service agency personnel to develop the social service directory for Lawrence, Kansas. We gratefully acknowledge the time and effort of the personnel from all of the agencies that helped to identify the problem-service categories. Special thanks go to Stephanie Mathews for her assistance in editing the final version of this book. The guidance and cooperation of all of these people made this work possible.

The preparation of an earlier version of this book was funded in part by a grant from the Kansas Board of Regents under Program IMPACT—Title I of the Higher Education Act of 1965 (Community Services and Continuing Education) to the authors at the Institute for Public Affairs and Community Development (now the Center for Public Affairs) at the University of Kansas.

R. Mark Mathews
Stephen B. Fawcett

Part I

DEVELOPING AN INFORMATION
AND REFERRAL SYSTEM

THE REFERRAL PROGRAM

This book is designed to assist you in establishing an information and referral system in your community. In developing this book, we have attempted to carefully specify the "nuts and bolts" of a referral program in order to simplify the task of developing a new program.

WHAT IS IT?

The information and referral system described here is made up of four components.

1. A Social Service Directory. The heart of the information and referral system, the directory provides a listing of problems handled and services provided by local community service agencies. Chapters. 1 and 2 describe how to develop a social service directory.

2. An Interagency Feedback Loop. Feedback to agencies providing referrals helps insure quality information and referral services. In this system, feedback is made possible by a set of interagency referral forms. These forms serve four functions: (1) they provide a record of referrals provided by an agency; (2) they serve as a reminder of the appointment for the client; (3) they provide information on services needed by clients; and (4) they provide the referral agency with information on which services were actually received by the client. Therefore, the interagency referral form serves to assist the referral agency, the client, and the agency to which the client is referred. Chapter 3 describes a method for promoting interagency feedback.

3. Staff Training. Agency staff often require instruction in how to operate the newly developed information and referral system. Chapter 4 describes how to train community service workers in providing effective referrals. In addition, Part II of this book contains programmed training materials designed to teach staff members how to provide information and referral services.

4. Social Service Directory Updating. For an information and referral system to be useful for an extended period of time, a method for updating agency service information must be available. There are few things in life that are more frustrating than trying to use an out-of-date directory. Chapter 3 outlines suggestions for easy updating of the system.

These four components—the social service directory, an interagency feedback loop, staff training, and social service directory updating—make up this information and referral system.

IS THIS PROGRAM FOR MY COMMUNITY?

This section is designed to help you determine if an information and referral system is needed in your community. Program development efforts are time consuming and should not occur without due cause. Answers to the following three questions may help to determine whether this program is for you.

1. Is There Already an Adequate Referral System in the Community? If an adequate system for referring clients to social service agencies is already available, there is probably no need to set up a new system. If another local agency has a comprehensive and up-to-date referral system that is effective in matching a wide range of client problems with the most appropriate service agency, then perhaps the existing program can be adopted by your agency. It makes no sense to try to rediscover the wheel.

That said, determining the "adequacy" of information and referral services can be a sticky problem. It is as easy to decide that another agency's programs are inadequate as it is to determine that your own are quite acceptable (of course). One way to begin assessing the adequacy of the existing information and referral system is to ask questions of *clients:* Can you obtain information about which agencies handle which problems? Is this information accurate? Is the quality of information and referral consistent across service agencies in this city?

It is also important to ask questions of *service-givers* at other agencies: Do you know which agencies in the city handle each type of problem presented to you? Are information and referral skills widely shared by your agency staff or are you dependent on the stored knowledge of a few of your staff members? Is your agency's information about the service capabilities of other agencies up-to-date? Is it possible for you to obtain feedback on what happens to a client that you refer to another agency? If the answer to many of these questions is no, then perhaps your community would benefit from the information and referral system described in this book.

2. Is There a Client Mandate? This can be restated as "Who decided that this is a problem?" If clients and other service-givers do not share your opinion that information and referral services need improvement, a new information and referral system has little chance of adoption. Accordingly, to develop such a system would probably be a waste of time. Ask other service-givers if they would adopt the proposed information and referral system if it were available. An enthusiastic response would support plans for developing such a system.

3. Are Resources Available? Developing a comprehensive information and referral system—conducting agency interviews, preparing and editing a social service directory, and teaching staff members how to use the new system—requires a large investment of time and energy. It is reasonable to expect the project to require the services of a program developer working approximately 20 hours per week for 9 to 12 weeks. In addition, materials such as card files, index cards, paper, and access to a typewriter will also be needed. If the system is to be used by more than one agency, funds for printing will also be required.

If you have determined that there is a need for an information and referral system, a client mandate, and sufficient resources, then read on. The remainder of this section describes how the program was originally developed and provides an overview of the task of implementing this program in your community.

HOW WAS THIS PROGRAM DEVELOPED?

This book has evolved from our experiences with an information and referral program originally developed and operated in Lawrence, Kansas, a midwestern city of about 60,000 persons (Mathews and Fawcett, 1979b). Our involvement stemmed from complaints by the staff of various social service agencies about the inadequacy of information on the services provided by other local agencies, the frequency of inappropriate client referrals, and statements made by the local council of social service agencies identifying a need for improvement in information and referral services.

From our experience, we have found that the success of any community program is often directly related to the level of involvement of representatives of local community organizations. The adoption and use of a program can often depend on the involvement of indigenous people in the design of the program. If the innovation is coproduced, through consultation between the program development specialist and representatives of the community agencies, its usefulness may be increased. As local residents become involved in dialogue regarding community problems and their causes, the people become critical of conditions in their community and committed to the improvement of those conditions (Freire, 1970). Involvement in the coproduction of innovative community programs provides an opportunity for residents to participate in the development of their own communities. In addition, the increased involvement of community residents helps to insure that the program will meet the needs of the community. Therefore, we strongly recommend that you work closely with the on-line staff of a variety of social service agencies in the development of your information and referral system.

We have also found that social service agencies situated in areas from which their clients come are particularly effective in handling problems. Further, these agencies are often most effective when they employ persons drawn from the community (Hallowitz and Riessman, 1967). Therefore, an information and referral system might best be designed for use by helpers indigenous to the community to be served.

With the expanded use of nonprofessionals and volunteer staff, the importance of training nonprofessionals in relevant helping skills is increased (D'Augelli et al., 1976). This suggests the need for effective methods and materials designed to teach information and referral skills to indigenous community service workers. The training materials contained in this book were developed to teach service-givers the skills associated with using the social service directory, completing the interagency referral forms, and arranging client appointments. Each unit was prepared in a standardized format. The training sequence was designed so that it could be self-administered or administered by a member of the agency's staff. It involves having each trainee read a set of written instructions, complete a study guide, complete a number of written situational examples, practice the referral behaviors, and obtain feedback on performance. This procedure is followed for each lesson training how to provide information and referrals. This systematic approach to teaching skills was designed to increase the replicability of the procedures by trainers other than the designers of the system (Mathews and Fawcett, 1977a; Fawcett et al., 1980).

IS THE PROGRAM EFFECTIVE?

In an experimental demonstration, Mathews and Fawcett (1979c) found the lessons contained in this book to be effective in increasing the occurrence of specific referral behaviors performed by community service workers. The results showed an increase in performance of referral behaviors from a pretraining average of 20% to a posttraining average of 94%. In addition, this research indicated that training in how to provide a referral produced a simultaneous increase in the proportion of referrals provided to appropriate agencies. Appropriate referrals increased from a pretraining average of 44% to a post-training average of 100%.

HOW LONG DOES IT TAKE TO START A PROGRAM?

Our experience indicates that it would require a program coordinator, working one-half time on the referral program, approximately three months to develop an information and referral system and to train the staff of one agency how to use the system. Of course, you should expect the project to take longer if you are setting up a referral system in a very large urban area with many social services. Similarly, if, as program coordinator, you can devote only a small fraction of your time to setting up the program, it will also take longer.

The PERT chart below provides a representation of a 12-week time frame for developing the information and referral system.

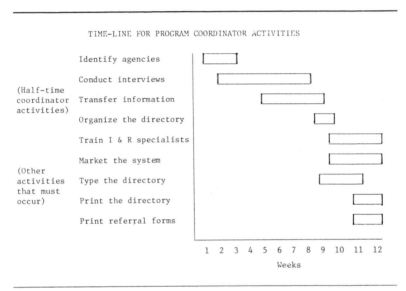

TIME-LINE FOR PROGRAM COORDINATOR ACTIVITIES

(Half-time coordinator activities)

Identify agencies

Conduct interviews

Transfer information

Organize the directory

Train I & R specialists

Market the system

(Other activities that must occur)

Type the directory

Print the directory

Print referral forms

1 2 3 4 5 6 7 8 9 10 11 12
Weeks

Chapter 1

GATHERING INFORMATION ABOUT LOCAL COMMUNITY SERVICES

IDENTIFYING SOCIAL SERVICE AGENCIES

Setting up an information and referral system for your community is a complex and time-consuming task. The first steps in developing a referral program are to identify the social service agencies located in your community and determine what services each agency offers. This chapter is designed to provide you with a variety of helpful hints to simplify the task of gathering information about local community services.

We have found that a good way to start your list of agencies is by writing down all of the local service agencies with which you have had previous contact. Share this list with other service-givers to obtain names of additional agencies. You can also check with your agency's listing of frequently called numbers for other agencies that might not have been mentioned. At this point, your goal is to come up with as comprehensive a list of agencies as you possibly can.

Another major source of information is the telephone directory. However, you should remember that the Yellow Pages may be only somewhat helpful, as its format was not designed for this purpose. So called Peoples' Yellow Pages, or other local directories, may also be useful in obtaining the names, addresses, and telephone numbers of existing social service agencies. Listed below are a number of information categories and service titles that may be helpful in

locating social service agencies in the telephone book. This list is
provided to give you some ideas about different ways that services
might be listed; it does not contain all possible listings.

Adoption	Homebound Services
Aging	Home Improvement
Alcoholism	Housing
Appliances	Housing Assistance
Birth Control	Information
Blindness	Information Services
Budgeting	Legal Assistance
Child Abuse	Meals
Childbirth	Medical
Childcare	Mental Health
Child Custody	Military
Child Welfare	Newsletters
Clothing	Photocopy Services
Community Action	Police
Community Mental Health	Police Problems
Community Programs	Preschools
Complaints	Programs for Special Populations
Counseling	Poverty Problems
Crisis Intervention	Rape Counseling
Disaster Relief	Recreation
Discrimination	Retirement
Drug Information	Self-Help Groups
Economic Assistance	Speech Problems
Elderly	Speech Therapists
Emergency Assistance	Substance Abuse
Employment	Transportation
Financial Assistance	Utility Problems
Food	Venereal Disease
Form Completion	Veterans Services
Furniture	Volunteers
Handicapped	Welfare Problems
Health	Welfare Programs
Hearing Evaluation	Youth Programs
Hearing Problems	

We have found that it is helpful to make a list of potential helping agencies that should be contacted. Below is a sample list of agencies to be interviewed:

Existing Social Service Agencies

Agency Name	Address	Phone	Interview Appointment
Red Cross	1406 Tennessee	961-9475	July 7, 3:30 w/Robin Burgess
Helping Hand	124 West 11th	935-7734	July 8, 4:15 w/Mrs. Miller

This listing of community agencies is the basis for gathering information about the services offered in your community. Therefore, it is important to identify all of the existing agencies in the community.

On the next page we have provided a form for you to start your own list of local service agencies. You can begin working on your information and referral system by starting a list of agencies here.

Social Service Agencies

Agency Name	Address	Phone	Interview Appointment
1.			
2.			
3.			
4.			
5.			
6.			
7.			
8.			
9.			
10.			
11.			
12.			
13.			
14.			
15.			
16.			
17.			
18.			
19.			
20.			
21.			
22.			
23.			
24.			
25.			

ARRANGING AN APPOINTMENT

When you are ready to begin conducting agency interviews, a good place to start is by arranging an appointment with a knowledgeable employee of the social service agency. Arranging an appointment will help to reduce the time you spend in waiting rooms. Making an appointment will also increase the likelihood that you will have the full attention and cooperation of the person you are interviewing. Service agency personnel are very busy, and without an appointment, you may be perceived as an unwanted intruder taking up valuable time.

We recommend six activities to arrange an appointment: list the agency's name, address, and phone number; call the agency; identify yourself; explain your purpose; request an appointment with a knowledgeable staff member; and record the appointment time.

LIST THE AGENCY'S NAME, ADDRESS, AND TELEPHONE NUMBER

We suggest that you write the name, address, and phone number of the agency in the appropriate blanks at the top of an Agency Information Form. A blank copy of this form is included at the end of this unit and may be duplicated for your own use. The local telephone directory is, of course, a good source of the necessary information. Below is an example of how the agency's name, address, and phone number might look on the Agency Information Form:

AGENCY INFORMATION FORM

Agency Name: *Social and Rehabilitation Services (SRS)*	Hours of Operation:
Agency Address: *1421 E. 11th*	After Hours Number:
Agency Phone Number: *421-9286*	Age Criterion:
Appointments Accepted:	Economic Criterion:

Listing the agency's name, address, and phone number will help you to keep a record of which agencies you have contacted. In addition, the Agency Information Form will be used during the agency interview and should include this information. This will help to insure that you know which agency provided what information.

CALL THE AGENCY

Next, we recommend that you dial the agency's telephone number and wait for someone to answer the telephone. It is important to call the agency so that you can make an appointment with someone who works there.

IDENTIFY YOURSELF

When someone answers the telephone at the agency, we suggest that you make an initial greeting, state your name, and state the name of the agency or organization that you represent. Examples of ways to identify yourself include:

(1) "Hello, my name is Lynn Roberts and I'm from the Institute for Community Affairs at the University."
(2) "Hi, I'm Bob McRobert. I'm calling from Volunteers Incorporated."
(3) "Hello, this is Doris Marshall. I'm with the First Street Service Center."

Identifying yourself will let the agency staff member know who you are and the name of the organization that you represent.

STATE YOUR PURPOSE

Next, we recommend that you briefly state that you are attempting to develop a directory of community services. Below are some examples of ways to state your purpose:

(1) "We are trying to list all of the agencies in the community that provide services and what those services are."
(2) "I'm working on a directory of services offered in the community."

Stating your purpose will let the person know why you are calling and the kind of information that you will need.

REQUEST AN APPOINTMENT WITH A
KNOWLEDGEABLE STAFF MEMBER

We recommend that you ask for an appointment with someone who knows all of the services offered by the agency. You should make sure that the appointment time is convenient for the person. It is also important to arrange for at least 30 minutes with the person. Some larger agencies may not have one person who will be able to describe the entire operation. In this case, you should arrange separate appointments with each appropriate staff member. Below are examples of how to request an appointment with a knowledgeable staff member:

(1) "I'd like to make an appointment to meet with someone who knows about all of the services offered by your agency."
(2) "Could I arrange an appointment with one of your staff members to discuss the services offered by your agency?"
(3) "May I schedule an appointment with someone on your staff who could describe the services offered by your agency?"

Arranging an appointment with a knowledgeable staff member will enable you to speak with someone who can describe the services offered by the agency. It is important to allow at least 30 minutes for the meeting because less time may result in incomplete or inaccurate information.

RECORD THE APPOINTMENT TIME

After you have arranged the appointment, we recommend that you write the name of the person, the place, and the date of the interview on your list of agencies or on an appointment calendar. Examples of ways to record the appointment time include:

(1) "Joe Smith, 3:30 p.m., The Heart Association, 4/12/77."
(2) "Dr. Williams, 8:00 a.m., Headstart, 12/2/78."

Recording the appointment time on your list of agencies or on an appointment calendar will help insure that you remember the appointment. If you are not able to be at the agency for the scheduled appointment time or if you are going to be late, you should always call the agency *before* the scheduled appointment and arrange for a new time. This courtesy helps insure the cooperation of the agency staff.

The following interaction shows how all of the activities involved in arranging an appointment for an agency interview might fit together. For our example, Julie Howell is a community service

worker who has volunteered to develop an information and referral
system for the United Way of St. Louis. She has completed a list of
all of the known service agencies in St. Louis and is ready to call for
her first interview. The first agency she plans to contact is the
Services for Aging, 311 N.W. Tennessee, at 611-9127. Julie calls
the agency and after the telephone rings twice:

Services for Aging: Good morning, Services for Aging. May I
help you?

Julie: Hello, my name is Julie Howell. I'm working for the St. Louis
United Way. We are currently trying to develop an information and
referral system that lists all of the services that are provided by
agencies here in town. I'd like to make an appointment to talk with
someone from the Services for Aging about the services that you offer.

Services for Aging: Well, Julie, my name is Ronn Walters. I'm the
program director here, so I guess that I'd be the person that you need to
talk to.

Julie: Great! When would be a good time for me to come in to talk with
you?

Services for Aging: How about tomorrow at 3:00?

Julie: That will be fine with me. Could you allow for us to meet for 30
minutes to an hour? That way we'll be sure to have enough time to
cover everything.

Services for Aging: Sure, I'll put you down from 3:00 to 4:00, Julie.

Julie: Thanks very much, Mr. Walters. I'll see you tomorrow at 3:00.

After hanging up the phone, Julie wrote "3:00 p.m., September 22,
Mr. Walters" across from "Services for Aging" on her agency list.
    In summary, to arrange an appointment, we recommend the
following activities:

(1) list the agency's name, address, and telephone number
(2) call the agency
(3) identify yourself
(4) state your purpose
(5) request an appointment with a knowledgeable staff member
(6) record the appointment time.

These activities should be helpful in arranging an appointment for an interview. The following page contains a blank Agency Information Form for your use. We recommend that you use this type of form to collect information about each of the agencies that you contact. Feel free to photocopy the form or to type new ones for your use.

Because most people learn best by doing, we suggest that you put your learning into action. You can try out the skills involved in scheduling an interview by contacting one of the agencies on your list of existing social service agencies. To make this first contact as pleasant as possible, you might schedule your first appointment with a staff member of an agency with which you have previously had contact.

AGENCY INFORMATION FORM

Agency Name: Hours of Operation:
Agency Address: After Hours Number:
Agency Phone Number: Age Criterion:
Appointments Accepted for Clients: Economic Criterion:
   YES [   ]   NO [   ]

                              Other Eligibility Requirements:

DIRECT SERVICES OFFERED	SPECIFIC PROBLEMS HANDLED	AVAILABLE IF:	CONTACT PERSON

CONDUCTING THE INTERVIEW

The information obtained during an agency interview is the basis of the information and referral system. If this information is inaccurate or incomplete, the referral system will be of little value. Therefore, your care in conducting agency interviews will be reflected in the referral system.

We recommend a total of 16 steps in conducting an agency interview. These steps will be described in two phases—collecting background information about the agency and obtaining information about the services provided by the agency. To collect background information about the agency we recommend the following: identify yourself; state that you need information; request the hours of operation; ask if appointments are accepted; ask about after hours assistance; ask about any age criteria; ask about any economic criteria; and ask if there are other eligibility requirements.

IDENTIFY YOURSELF

We suggest that you arrive at the agency at the prearranged appointment time and introduce yourself. The introduction should include your name, affiliation, and the purpose of your visit. For example, you might identify yourself by saying: "Hello, Mr. Goodman. I'm Susan Davis from Helping Hands. I'm here to talk with you about your organization." This statement will remind the person that you have an appointment, who you are, and the purpose of your visit.

STATE THAT YOU NEED INFORMATION

We have found that it is useful to explain that you will be asking a number of questions about the organization and its services. Below is an example of one way to state that you need information: "I need some information about the services offered by the Community Mental Health Center." This kind of statement helps to clarify the purpose of the meeting and sets the agenda.

REQUEST THE HOURS OF OPERATION

We recommend that you begin the interview by asking when the agency is open. You should write this information on the Agency

Information Form beside HOURS OF OPERATION. For example, you might say:

(1) "The first thing I need to know is what hours you are open."
(2) "The first question I have is, what are your hours of operation?"

Below is a sample Agency Information Form used in interviewing the South Side Center. The hours of operation have been recorded in the appropriate place.

AGENCY INFORMATION FORM

Agency Name: *South Side Center*   Hours of Operation: *9am-4pm*
                                            M-F

Agency Address: *1401 S. Hampton*   After Hours Number:
Agency Phone Number: *361-9141*   Age Criterion:
Appointments Accepted for Clients: Economic Criterion:
   YES [   ]   NO [   ]

                                        Other Eligibility Requirements:

ASK IF APPOINTMENTS ARE ACCEPTED

We suggest that you ask if the agency is willing to schedule appointment times for their clients. This is important information, as many agencies only work on a first-come, first-served basis. For example: "Does your agency accept appointments?" If the American Cancer Association does accept appointments, the Agency Information Form might look like this:

AGENCY INFORMATION FORM

Agency Name: *American*   Hours of Operation: *9am-4pm*
  Cancer Assn.   *M & F*
Agency Address: *1201 West 6th*   After Hours Number:
Agency Phone Number: *862-6161*   Age Criterion:
Appointments Accepted for Clients: Economic Criterion:
   YES [x]   NO [   ]

                                        Other Eligibility Requirements:

ASK ABOUT AFTER-HOURS ASSISTANCE

We feel that it is also important to check whether clients can receive help after the agency's normal hours of operation. If after-hours assistance is available, write the telephone number and name of the person to be called on the Agency Information Form. If no after-hours assistance is offered by the agency, then write "None" in the space provided. You might ask about after-hours assistance by saying: "Is there assistance available here after hours?" Below is an example of what would be recorded if the County Hearing Clinic offered after-hours assistance:

AGENCY INFORMATION FORM

Agency Name: *County Hearing Clinic*	Hours of Operation: *1-5 pm F*
Agency Address: *421 Maine*	After Hours Number: *Bob Johnson 351-3198*
Agency Phone Number: *842-9229*	Age Criterion:
Appointments Accepted for Clients: YES [x] NO [ ]	Economic Criterion:
	Other Eligibility Requirements:

REQUEST AGE CRITERION

Because many agencies are funded to work only with a certain age group, we recommend that you ask if the agency's services are restricted to (or designed primarily for) one age group. Write the information on the Agency Information Form after the age criterion heading. For example, you might say:

(1) "Do you have an age criterion?"
(2) "Is there any restriction on the age of clients your agency can serve?"

An example of one agency with an age criterion is provided below:

AGENCY INFORMATION FORM

Agency Name: *Services for Aging*	Hours of Operation: *8am-5pm M-F*
Agency Address: *311 N.W. Tennessee*	After Hours Number: *None*
Agency Phone Number: *611-9127*	Age Criterion: *All services for people over 55 yrs of age*
Appointments Accepted for Clients: YES [x] NO [ ]	Economic Criterion:
	Other Eligibility Requirements:

This information is very important. If the referral directory does not note the age criterion of programs, people too young to be eligible for services for the elderly might be sent to the agency. Similarly, an adult might be sent to an agency that can only work with adolescents.

REQUEST ECONOMIC CRITERION

We also recommend that you ask if the agency has any economic guidelines that they must follow. This information should also be noted if the agency has no specific restrictions, but is designed for low-income or middle-income families. For example:

(1) "Do your clients have to meet any economic criterion?"
(2) "Are there any restrictions on the income of clients served here?"

Below is an example of an economic criterion:

AGENCY INFORMATION FORM

Agency Name: *Emergency Service Council*

Agency Address: *4711 Ohio*

Agency Phone Number: *961-4948*

Appointments Accepted for Clients:
YES [x]   NO [ ]

Hours of Operation: *9am-3pm M-F*

After Hours Number: *None*

Age Criterion: *None*

Economic Criterion:
Economically disadvantaged

Other Eligibility Requirements:

ASK ABOUT OTHER ELIGIBILITY REQUIREMENTS

Finally, we suggest that you ask if the agency's services are restricted in any other way. This could include such requirements as a program being restricted to only court-adjudicated males, only single parents, only children with learning disabilities, or only people that live in a specific neighborhood. Below are examples of ways to ask about other eligibility requirements:

(1) "Are there *any* restrictions on the clients that may be served by your agency?"
(2) "Are there any other eligibility requirements your clients must meet?"
(3) "Are there any restrictions on your clients, such as where they live, marital status, physical condition, or anything like that?"

Below is an example of an Agency Information Form for an agency that has special eligibility requirements:

AGENCY INFORMATION FORM

Agency Name: *Parents without Partners*

Hours of Operation: *6-8pm M-F*

Agency Address: *412 Ohio Rm 313*

After Hours Number: *None*

Agency Phone Number: *842-4111*

Age Criterion: *None*

Appointments Accepted for Clients:
YES [ ]   NO [x]

Economic Criterion: *None*

Other Eligibility Requirements: *Must be a single parent*

Of course, it is important to be polite throughout the interview. Common courtesies, such as saying please and thank you, will do much to set a pleasant tone for the meeting. Further, a polite and positive interaction may help enhance the interagency cooperation that is essential to an effective social service network.

The following narrative is provided to illustrate how the first part of an agency interview might progress. In this example our program developer, Julie Howell, is interviewing Rhoda Barnett from the Transit Authority's Transportation Program for the Handicapped.

Julie: Good morning, I'm Julie Howell from the United Way. I've come to talk with you about the services that your organization provides. I'll need to ask you several questions about the Transportation Program for the Handicapped.

Rhoda: Fine, I'll be glad to help out. Would you have a seat, please?

Julie: Thank you. Rhoda, what are your hours of operation?

Rhoda: Well, our vans run from 7:00 a.m. to 8:30 p.m. seven days a week.

Julie: Do you accept appointments?

Rhoda: Yes. As a matter of fact, we only offer our services if the client has made an appointment at least one day in advance.

Julie: Do you have any after-hours assistance?

Rhoda: No, we can only afford to operate the program during the hours that the van runs. However, we do have a code-a-phone so that people can leave a message for the drivers.

Julie: Do you have any age or economic criterion for the use of your services?

Rhoda: No. Our only criteria is that the person must have a physical disability.

Julie: Okay, so there aren't any restrictions about where people live or anything like that?

Rhoda: Well, I'm glad you mentioned that. We do have one other restriction. We can't take the vans out of the county.

At this point in the interview, Julie's Agency Information Form would look like this:

AGENCY INFORMATION FORM

Agency Name: *St. Louis Transit Authority—Handicapped Program*

Hours of Operation: *7am-8:30pm M-S*

Agency Address: *1835 W. 37th*

After Hours Number: *Leave phone messages at 941-8012*

Agency Phone: *941-8012*

Age Criterion: *None*

Appointments Accepted for Clients:
YES [x]   NO [ ]

Economic Criterion: *None*

Other Eligibility Requirements: *Physical disability & only in-county transportation*

In summary, to gather background information about the agency we suggest that you do the following:

(1) identify yourself
(2) state that you need information
(3) request the hours of operation
(4) ask if appointments are accepted
(5) ask if after-hours assistance is available
(6) request age criterion
(7) request economic criterion
(8) ask if there are other eligibility requirements.

To obtain information about the agency's services, we recommend that you perform nine steps: provide a sample list; list each direct service; list the specific problems handled; list any restrictions; list the person to contact; read back the complete list; ask about specialized referrals; request additional help; and state your appreciation.

PROVIDE A SAMPLE LIST

We have found that it is often very useful to provide the person that you are interviewing with a list of possible problems and services. (A sample list is provided at the end of this chapter. Feel free to use it as it is or to add to it for your own use.) As you hand the sample list to the person, we recommend that you describe its purpose. You should explain that the list contains examples of the type of services and problems that you plan to list in the referral system (that is, specific, direct services). You should also tell the person to read the list and select the problems handled and services offered by his or her agency. Finally, it is very important to explain that the list is not exhaustive. That is, she or he should feel free to mention problems handled or services offered by the agency that are not included on the list. Examples of ways to describe the purpose of the list of problems and services are provided below:

(1) "Here is a list of possible client problems and potential services. Would you examine the list and let me know which problems you handle. Also, please mention any services you offer that aren't listed."
(2) "We've made a list of possible services that you can look over. As you can see, we are interested in finding out what specific, direct services you offer. Please mention any services that are not listed as well as those that are."

A list of appropriate examples helps to structure the interview and to reduce the chance that you will be told that the agency "does everything that the client needs." The list should help to show the person what type of services you plan to list in your directory.

LIST EACH DIRECT SERVICE

We recommend that you write down all of the direct services offered by the agency. This information can be included on the Agency Information Form under the heading Direct Services Offered. It is important to list only direct services, those services provided directly by that agency. It is also important to be specific in your description of services. For example, if the agency provides *referrals* for clients with alcohol and drug problems and operates a transportation program for the elderly, you should *list only the transportation service* under "Direct Services Offered." It is important to be specific and to list only the direct services since a client's time is wasted by being referred to one agency only to receive another referral. The more specific you are about the services that are offered, the easier it will be to use the social service directory.

LIST THE SPECIFIC PROBLEMS HANDLED

You should also write a description of the specific problems that are handled by each of the direct services offered by the agency. This more detailed information should be listed under the heading Problems Handled on the Agency Information Form. Below are several examples:

DIRECT SERVICE	**PROBLEMS HANDLED**
Transportation for elderly	Rides to and from the doctor's office, hospital, or grocery store.
Housing assistance	For people who need temporary housing (up to one week)
Emergency medicine	For people who need a prescription filled, but can't afford to pay for it.

This information will be helpful for the person who is trying to determine what agency can help solve a client's specific problem.

LIST ANY RESTRICTIONS

At this point, we have found that it is important to find out about any restrictions on each of the specific services that are offered by the agency. This involves writing the who, when, where, how much, how often, and cost of each direct service under the heading Available If on the Agency Information Form. One agency that we interviewed offered free lunches. However, a separate question was needed to prompt the staff member to mention that the program was for the low-income, elderly residents of the city; that the program for free lunches was offered only Monday through Friday; and that clients could participate as often as they wanted. This information was important, because the agency itself was open seven days a week and offered other services to all age groups. Because different services offered by one agency can have their own restrictions, it is important to ask about restrictions for *each* program or service.

LIST THE CONTACT PERSON

We suggest that you ask if any one individual is responsible for the delivery of each service. Some agencies split their operation so that each staff member has specific responsibilities for a particular program. If this is the case, it is important to list the contact person for each service. This information will be valuable in trying to schedule an appointment for a client with the person who is responsible for the service that the client needs.

This process of listing each direct service, listing the specific problems handled, listing restrictions on each service, and listing the contact person, *should be repeated for each service offered by the agency.* Once the person that you are interviewing has gone through all of the services that the agency offers, we suggest that you review the services as shown below.

READ BACK THE LIST OF SERVICES

We recommend that, once all of the agency's services have been listed and explained, you read back the entire list of services and request additions or corrections. Below are two examples of ways to read back the list of services:

(1) "The services you offer include: emergency food, emergency medical prescriptions, clothing, and welfare counseling. Have we left anything out?"

(2) "The services that I have listed for you are transportation for the handicapped and a program to help the handicapped learn new job-related skills. Is there anything else we should include?"

Reading the list of services back to the person that you are interviewing will provide an opportunity for the person to mention new services or clarify the services that have been listed.

ASK ABOUT SPECIALIZED REFERRALS

We have also found it to be useful to ask about any special types of referral programs that the organization might offer. Some agencies maintain an up-to-date, extensive listing of specialized services: that is, services or agencies directed toward specific populations (for example, a list of day care centers); lists of services that change frequently (e.g., babysitters); or listings that are important, but not in frequent general demand or are too extensive to include in your referral directory (e.g., psychiatrists and state agencies). Examples of some specialized referral programs include listings of babysitters, day care centers, nursing homes, public schools, private physicians, psychologists, psychiatrists, federal agencies, state agencies, and fraternal organizations.

Many indirect services, such as specialized referral capabilities, may be valuable to the community, and thus to the clients served by your referral system. For the most part, it is important to refer your clients to an agency where they can obtain the direct service that they require. However, to maintain an up-to-date listing of every possible service would be burdensome (if not impossible) and may not be worth the great effort required (if the problem handled is not common). This is especially true if another agency devotes considerable time and effort to handling information pertaining to specific problems. The distinction may seem difficult to make— perhaps an example would help to clarify the issue: There is no reason for every agency to maintain an up-to-date listing of local babysitters. However, it is important for every agency to know which agency does maintain an up-to-date list of local babysitters.

REQUEST HELP IN IDENTIFYING ADDITIONAL AGENCIES

Before you finish the interview, it might be useful to ask the person that you are interviewing to look over your list of social service agencies and suggest the names of any agencies that have been omitted. If any new agencies are mentioned, be sure to add them to your list. This information can be useful in insuring a complete directory of social services.

STATE YOUR APPRECIATION

To finish the interview, we recommend that you thank the person for his or her time and effort. At the same time you can let him or her know when you expect the information and referral directory to be complete and when it will be available. Examples of ways to state your appreciation include:

(1) "Thanks so much for your time and help in describing your services. The directory should be completed some time next month. I'll be back in touch to let you know when it's available."

(2) "I appreciate all the help you've given us on this project. Once the directory is printed, I'll get a copy of it to you. I hope it will be sometime this summer."

A genuine expression of gratitude will help maintain a basis for further collaboration.

The following narrative is provided to illustrate how this part of the interview might sound. In this example, Julie is interviewing a staff member from the Rape Victim Support Service (RVSS).

Julie: Here is a list of the types of services that we're interested in finding out about. I'd appreciate it if you would look over the list and tell me about any of these, or any other services, that you offer here at RVSS.

RVSS: The first program I see here that we offer is Counseling. I'm sure you know, that's our primary service.

Julie: Okay, exactly what types of problems do you offer counseling for?

RVSS: Our services include the initial crisis counseling after the rape or attempted rape. We often follow-up with marital, pregnancy, or psychological counseling for the problems that can occur after a sexual assault.

Julie: Are there any restrictions on your counseling services?

RVSS: No, there aren't any time, age, or income restrictions for the counseling.

Julie: Is there a specific person to contact?

RVSS: Each case is handled by one of our 15 RVSS counselors. However, the initial call and contact must be through our main office, which is staffed 24 hours per day.

Julie: Okay, do you see any other services on the list that you offer?

RVSS: Well, one of our counselors is a lawyer who offers free legal assistance to any of our clients. This legal assistance is for any problem that might be related to the rape.

Julie: Who should be contacted for this service?

RVSS: Again, we prefer to have the initial call come to the main office.

Julie: Any other services on the list, or that you offer that we don't have listed?

RVSS: No, that's about it.

Julie: So the services that you offer include rape counseling, marital counseling, pregnancy counseling, psychological counseling, and legal assistance. All for rape victims.

RVSS: Yes, that's about it.

Julie: Do you handle any special types of referrals or offer any specialized indirect services?

RVSS: We keep a file on all of the rape counseling programs that are operating in the nation. In that way, if someone is molested here, we can help out immediately and also provide a referral to a program nearest to the victim's home.

Julie: You've been a great help. Would you mind looking over this list of local agencies and telling me if we've left anyone out?

RVSS: You have listed all of the agencies that I know of, this really looks quite complete.

Julie: Thanks. I appreciate your help with the referral program. I expect that the system will be complete by this October. If you're interested in getting a copy of the directory, we will be selling them for about $25. I'll be getting back to everyone that is listed in the directory as soon as it's ready.

In summary, the steps involved in obtaining information about the agency's services include:

(1) provide a sample list
(2) list each direct service
(3) list the specific problems handled
(4) list any restrictions
(5) list the contact person
(6) read back the complete list of services
(7) ask about specialized referrals
(8) request additional help
(9) state your appreciation.

We hope the activities described in this chapter will be helpful to you in conducting the type of agency interviews that will produce accurate and complete information. The next few pages contain a listing of potential problem and service categories that you can use while you conduct the interviews.

Now that you have completed this chapter, we suggest that you start conducting interviews of the social service agencies in your community. You are now well on the way to having a new social service directory.

POTENTIAL PROBLEM/SERVICE CATEGORIES

ABUSE AND ASSAULT

ADDICTION (see Alcohol and drug-related services)

ADOPTION

ADULT EDUCATION

AGING
  –books
  –financial assistance
  –home improvement
  –homemaking and chores
  –housing
  –jobs/volunteer
  –meals
  –medical
  –nursing home placement
  –nursing home visits
  –telephone reassurance
  –transportation
  –yard work

ALCOHOL AND DRUG-RELATED SERVICES
  –detoxification
  –detoxification transportation
  –counseling for family
  –information
  –in-patient programs
  –out-patient programs
  –transitional care

AMBULANCE

APPLIANCES
  –donation
  –needed

BABYSITTING REFERRALS

BATTERED WOMEN (see Abuse and Assault)

BIRTH CONTROL
  –counseling
  –information
  –medical

BLIND OR VISUALLY IMPAIRED

BLOOD

BUDGETING

CHILD ABUSE
  –legal complaints

CHILDBIRTH
  –education

CHILD CARE

CHILD CUSTODY

CHILD HEALTH AND NUTRITION

CHILD WELFARE

CIVIL DEFENSE

CIVIL RIGHTS (see Discrimination)

CLOTHING
  –donations
  –needed

COMMUNITY ACTION

COMMUNITY DEVELOPMENT

COMMUNITY MENTAL HEALTH

COMMUNITY PROGRAMS
COMPLAINTS
  –landlord/tenant
  –legal
  –merchandise
  –police problems
  –repair/service
  –sanitation
  –school problems
CONSUMER   PROBLEMS
  (see Complaints)
CONVALESCENT   CARE
  (see Nursing Homes)
COUNSELING
  –alcohol
  –budget
  –career and vocational
  –child abuse
  –crisis
  –divorce
  –drug
  –employment
  –financial
  –for the deaf
  –legal
  –premarital
  –poverty
  –pregnancy
  –psychological
  –rape
  –school problems
  –suicide
  –welfare
CRISIS INTERVENTION
DAY CARE
DEAF (see Hearing)
DISABLED (see Blind, Hearing, or Handicapped)

DISASTER RELIEF
DISCRIMINATION
  –education
  –employment
  –housing
DRUG ABUSE (see Alcohol
  and drug-related services)

ECONOMIC ASSISTANCE
  –disability checks
EDUCATION
  –financial assistance
  –G.E.D.
  –vocational rehabilitation
EDUCATIONAL   ASSIST-
  ANCE
  –homemaking
  –living skills
  –mentally retarded
  –physically handicapped
  –tutoring
ELDERLY (see Aging)
EMERGENCY ASSISTANCE
  –food
  –general
  –housing
EMOTIONAL PROBLEMS
  (see Mental Health)
EMPLOYMENT SERVICES
  –placement
  –testing
  –training
  –transportation
  –youth
EYE (see Blind or Visually Impaired)
FAMILY PLANNING (see
  Birth Control)

FINANCIAL ASSISTANCE
- aid to dependent children
- budget counseling
- general assistance
- supplemental security income

FOOD
- emergency
- wholesale

FORM COMPLETION

FOSTER CARE

FURNITURE
- donation
- needed

GERONTOLOGY (see Aging)

HANDICAPPED

HEALTH

HEARING PROBLEMS
- adults
- children

HEART

HOMEBOUND SERVICES

HOME ECONOMICS

HOME IMPROVEMENT

HOMEMAKER SERVICES

HOME REPAIR

HOSPITALS

HOUSING
- disabled
- elderly
- mentally retarded

HOUSING ASSISTANCE
- disabled
- elderly
- low income
- students
- temporary

IMMUNIZATIONS

INFORMATION
- federal programs

INFORMATION SERVICES
- local skills clubs
- poverty problems
- rape
- student

JOBS (see Employment Services)

LEGAL ASSISTANCE

LIBRARY

MEALS
- elderly

MEDICAL
- aides for home health
- assistance
- children
- drug overdose
- financial assistance
- immunizations
- medicare
- occupational therapy
- physical therapy
- premarital exam
- prescriptions
- therapists
- transportation

MENTAL HEALTH

MENTAL RETARDATION

MILITARY SERVICES (see Veteran services)

MINORITY SERVICES

NEWSLETTER

NURSING HOMES

NUTRITION

OLDER CITIZENS (see Aging)

PARENTS' GROUPS

PHOTOCOPY SERVICE

PHYSICALLY HANDICAPPED

POLICE PROBLEMS
- complaints

POVERTY PROGRAMS
PREGNANCY
PRESCHOOLS
PROBATION AND PAROLE
PROTECTIVE SERVICES
RAPE COUNSELING
RECREATION
RELIGION (referral service)
RENT PROBLEMS (see complaints)
RETARDED
RETIRED PERSONS (see Aging)
RETIREMENT HOMES (see Aging)
RUNAWAYS
SAFETY
SCHOOLS
SELF-HELP GROUP
    –friendship
SENIOR CITIZENS (see Aging)
SHELTERED WORKSHOPS
SPEECH PROBLEMS
    –children
    –therapists

SUBSTANCE ABUSE (see Alcohol and Drug-Related Services)

TRANSPORTATION
    –in town
    –out of town

UTILITY PROBLEMS

VENEREAL DISEASE
VETERANS SERVICES
    –compensation/pensions
VISITING NURSE
VOCATIONAL EDUCATION
VOLUNTEERS

WELFARE PROBLEMS
WELFARE PROGRAMS
WOMEN
    –counseling
    –discrimination
    –rape
    –support groups
YOUTH

Chapter 2

ORGANIZING THE
SOCIAL SERVICE DIRECTORY

The social service directory is the heart of the information and referral system. The directory contains all of the information collected during social service agency interviews. The ease with which the directory can be used will often determine the success of the referral program. Our goal in this chapter is to describe a format for social service directories that we have found to be both effective and efficient. In addition, we will describe the step-by-step process involved in organizing such a directory from the notes that you have obtained in the agency interviews.

The social service directory contains the list of services offered and problems handled by local community service agencies. It is designed to provide all of the information required for a community service worker to select the appropriate agency for a client referral. The directory enables the staff member to provide appropriate referrals without memorizing all of the services offered in the community.

The information and referral system that we initially developed for Lawrence, Kansas, used a Rolodex-type card file for the social service directory. The card file has four distinct advantages. First, it is handy; information printed on 3 x 5 Rolodex cards can easily be arranged and stored. Second, an alphabetized card file permits efficient retrieval of information. Third, unlike scattered notes about agencies, the card file helps prevent the loss of needed information.

Fourth, unlike a bound manual, the file is easily updated. A small loose-leaf binder could be substituted for the card file, retaining many of these advantages. In addition, the loose-leaf binder directory would be easier and less expensive to duplicate. This text will discuss the procedures for developing a card file directory. Many of the basic procedures will be useful if you choose to use a loose-leaf binder for your directory.

The social service directory consists of three sections: an index, a set of problem-service cards, and a set of agency cards. The index lists all of the problem and service categories contained in the social service directory. These problem and service categories (such as "Alcoholism Counseling" or "Emergency Assistance") provide a handy reference for problems experienced by, and services available to, your clients. The categories for an individual directory should be developed directly from the services offered in that particular community. The index allows social service workers to locate relevant problem-service categories quickly and easily.

The problem-service cards provide information about each service offered in the community. Each card lists the direct services offered, the specific problems handled, any restrictions to the service, and the agency (or agencies) offering the service. The cards provide information that will be useful for determining whether the service offered is appropriate for the client's problem.

The third section of the directory contains the agency cards. These cards list the agency's name, address, phone number, office hours, eligibility requirements, policies regarding appointments, and the name of a contact person in the agency (if available). A separate card is used for each agency that provides a service listed in the directory.

Thus, the three elements of the directory are the index, problem-service cards, and agency cards. These components facilitate labelling the client's service needs, finding information concerning services provided in the community, and identifying an appropriate agency.

There are several tasks involved in organizing the social service directory. First, the information must be transferred from the Agency Information Forms (described in Chapter 1) to 3 x 5 cards. Next, the cards must be edited, organized, typed, and printed. This chapter describes how to perform each of these tasks.

TRANSFERRING INFORMATION TO THE
SOCIAL SERVICE DIRECTORY

We have found that transferring the information obtained during agency interviews to the social service directory requires the following steps: completing an agency card, listing each direct service offered by the agency on a separate card, describing the client problem(s) handled, describing any restrictions to the service, and writing the name of the agency to contact.

COMPLETE AN AGENCY CARD

We have found that the following information should be included on a card that describes the social service agency: the agency's name, address, phone number, and office hours; the name of a contact person (if available); eligibility requirements; and whether appointments are accepted. This information should be provided in the same format for each social service agency listed in the directory. Below are two agency cards from the social service directory developed in Lawrence:

DOUGLAS COUNTY EXTENSION SERVICE

Address: 2110 Harper
Phone: 843-7058
Hours: 8:00-5:00 M-F
Contact Person: Earl VanMeter
Eligibility: Any resident of Douglas County—no charge for any
service.
Appointments: Yes

LEGAL AID SOCIETY

Address: 846½ Indiana
Phone: 843-4776
Hours: 9:00-12:00 and 1:00-5:00 M-F
Eligibility: Clients must be low-income residents of Douglas County.
No felony case can be handled.
Appointments: Yes

Completing an agency card for each social service organization will help insure that necessary agency information is readily available.

DESCRIBE THE DIRECT SERVICES OFFERED

We suggest that at the top of a clean, separate card you write a brief description of the service offered by the agency. If the agency offers more than one service, you should *list each service on a separate card*. This information can be drawn from the Direct Services Offered category of the Agency Information Form. This information should be written in all capital letters. If the service offered is a specfic service (e.g., prescriptions), that is a part of a general category of services (e.g., medical), write the specific service in lowercase letters and in parentheses following the general category. Many different agencies offer different types of counseling. Some specialize in legal counseling, others in welfare counseling, and still others in budget counseling. Therefore, if you are completing a service card for an agency that offers budget counseling, the card might look like this:

COUNSELING (Budget)

Other services are more general. In these cases, there is no need for additional information to be included in parentheses. For example, a card for assistance in form completion might look like this:

FORM COMPLETION

Providing a brief description of the service at the top of the card enables a social service worker to quickly locate the desired information.

DESCRIBE THE PROBLEMS HANDLED

A further description of the problems handled by each service should be included on the card. This information can be found on the Agency Information Form under the heading Specific Problems Handled. This information should be included on the problem-service card after the heading "Problem Handled." The information should be written in the form of what client problem or need can be met by the service listed at the top of the card. Below are examples of descriptions of problems handled by two different community services:

MEDICAL (Prescription)
Problem Handled: Need a prescription filled in an emergency, but cannot afford to pay for it.

FORM COMPLETION
Problem Handled: Need assistance in filling out welfare, social security, job application, and other forms.

Describing the problems handled by each service will help social service workers to provide appropriate referrals. The information will help to clarify whether the service will meet the client's actual needs.

DESCRIBE ANY RESTRICTIONS TO THE SERVICE

We suggest that you describe any restrictions to the service beneath the description of the problem handled. Information about restrictions on a service can be found on the Agency Information Form under the heading Available If. A sample problem-service card with a restriction to a service is provided below:

HOME IMPROVEMENT (Repairs)
Problem Handled: Need repairs on the electrical system, plumbing, roofing, painting, and so on.
Restrictions: For low-income homeowners only—not available to renters.

This information will help the service-giver using the referral system determine whether a client is eligible for a specific service.

WRITE THE NAME OF THE AGENCY
PROVIDING THE SERVICE

Each problem-service card should include the name of the agency (or agencies) that offer the particular service. If an agency has a particular contact person for the service, you should include the person's name after the agency's name. Below are two examples of completed problem service cards:

MEDICAL (prescriptions)

Problem Handled: Need a prescription handled in an emergency, by cannot afford to purchase the medicine.

Restrictions: Must be low-income resident of Douglas County.

Contact: Penn House

FORM COMPLETION

Problem Handled: Need assistance in filling out welfare, social security, job application, homestead relief forms, and so on.

Contact: Penn House
Salvation Army
Legal Aid (Bob Johnson)

This process, of completing problem-service cards and agency cards, *should be completed for each direct service and each specialized referral service offered by each agency in your community.* Accordingly, if there are a total of 50 social service agencies in your community, you should complete 50 agency cards. If these agencies offer a total of 200 different services, you should complete 200 problem-service cards.

In summary, the steps involved in transferring information to the social service directory include:

(1) complete an agency card
(2) list the direct services offered
(3) describe the problems handled
(4) describe any restrictions to the service
(5) list the agency providing the service.

EDITING THE SOCIAL SERVICE DIRECTORY

After staff members from each of the agencies in your community have been interviewed and all of the information has been transcribed onto cards for the social service directory, the file must be edited. This task is especially important if the agency interviews were conducted by several people or if the information was transferred to cards by more than one person. Variations in interviewing and recording style often result in confusion for the service giver trying to use the directory. In order to edit the social service directory, we recommend that you revise unclear descriptions and delete duplications.

REVISE UNCLEAR DESCRIPTIONS

We suggest that you read each problem-service card to be sure that the information is understandable and that its meaning is clear. You should rewrite any description that is unclear. If you have conducted the agency interviews and written the descriptions that appear on the problem-service cards, you might find it useful to have someone who is less familiar with the community's social services read over the directory. This fresh reading may be useful in spotting unclear descriptions. Below we have provided an example of a description of a service that we think might be unclear to many people trying to provide a referral. In this example, the listing is for an agency that has money available to purchase prescription medicine for patients who could not otherwise afford to buy the medicine prescribed for them.

MEDICAL PRESCRIPTIONS

Problem Handled: Program to provide medical prescriptions for those who could not otherwise afford them.

To someone who did not know exactly what the service was, it might look like the program provided the prescription itself (and not the money for the medicine that was prescribed). Therefore, a more appropriate description might be:

MEDICAL (Prescriptions Filled)

Problem Handled: For patients who have a medical prescription, but cannot afford to purchase the medicine.

Service givers using the social service directory will often know nothing about the services offered by another agency other than what is written on the cards. Therefore, if you ever think that a naive reader *might* have trouble understanding what the card means, then revise the card so that its meaning is clear.

DELETE DUPLICATIONS

In many communities, several social service agencies will offer the same service. If you find that your directory lists the same service more than once, you can reduce this duplication by listing all of the agencies that provide the same service on a single problem-service card. For example, if employment counseling is offered by the County Employment Office, a neighborhood service center, and the local CETA office, each of these agencies should be listed on one problem-service card for employment counseling. However, there should be a separate *agency card* for each agency.

ORGANIZING THE SOCIAL SERVICE DIRECTORY

The result of the previous steps should be an assortment of agency and problem-service cards. The last steps in developing a social service directory are designed to bring some method to this madness.

ALPHABETIZE THE CARDS

We recommend that you place the problem-service cards in alphabetical order. They should be alphabetized by the title of the service offered. In addition, the agency cards should be alphabetized by agency name. The outcome of this will be one set of service cards in alphabetical order and one set of agency cards in alphabetical order.

WRITE AN INDEX

We suggest that you next develop an index of the services offered in your community. As a first step, you can make an alphabetical list of the services included in the problem-service cards.

CROSS-LIST THE INDEX

After listing each of the services, we suggest that you read through the entire list looking for services that might be known by different titles. For any service that might be known by a different title, add that new title to the index as a cross-listing. For cross listings, we have found it useful to write "See (the title of the service as it appears on the problem-service card)" beside the cross-listings. This lets the service giver know to which card she/he should turn. For example, a client might come to your agency and request help finding an adult education class, a G.E.D. course, or a high school equivalency class. Similarly, immunizations might be thought of as a medical problem, immunizations, or shots. If a free vaccination service is listed in the social service directory under Medical (Immunizations), your index should contain at least the following entries (of course, they would appear in alphabetical order throughout the index):

(1) IMMUNIZATIONS (see MEDICAL, Immunizations)
(2) MEDICAL, Immunizations
(3) MEDICAL, Problems (see MEDICAL, Immunizations)
(4) SHOTS (see MEDICAL, Immunizations).

As you read through the list of services offered, try to imagine all of the possible ways that services could be cross-listed. The goal of the index is to make it easier for staff members to match a client's problem to a service offered in the community. Therefore, the more ways that the index is cross-listed, the easier the task.

The following box contains an example of what a portion of the index might look like after it has been completed and transferred to a series of 3 x 5 cards.

ELDERLY (see AGING)

EMERGENCY ASSISTANCE
    food
    general
    housing

EMOTIONAL PROBLEMS (see MENTAL HEALTH)

EMPLOYMENT SERVICES
    placement
    testing
    training
    transportation
    youth

EYE (see BLIND OR VISUALLY IMPAIRED)

FAMILY PLANNING (see BIRTH CONTROL)

FOOD
    emergency (see EMERGENCY ASSISTANCE, Food)

FOSTER CARE

FURNITURE
    donation
    needed

GERONTOLOGY (see AGING)

TYPING AND PRINTING THE
SOCIAL SERVICE DIRECTORY

The final step in developing a social service directory is to type and print the directory. This is a time-consuming task in itself. Each card must be typed and proofread for accuracy. If the social service directory is to be used by more than one service-giver, multiple copies will be needed. Because printing costs are often based on the size of the order, the cost per copy generally decreases as the number of copies ordered increases. Therefore, you might find that the more copies of the directory you have printed, the cheaper it will be per copy. To determine the cost of the directory that you have developed, you should estimate the number of directories that will be required, compute the number of cards to be printed in each directory, and check with local printers for cost estimates. Of course, you should then have the materials printed by the printer that is both reliable and inexpensive.

To summarize, the steps required to finalize the social service directory are:

(1) revise any unclear descriptions
(2) delete duplications
(3) alphabetize the cards
(4) write an index
(5) cross-list the index
(6) type and print the social service directory.

Chapter 3

PROMOTING INTERAGENCY FEEDBACK

Feedback from the participating organizations is required to maintain high-quality referral services. Without feedback from the helping agency (i.e., the agency to which the client is referred), there is little chance to find out if the client ever arrived for assistance or received the services for which he or she was referred. This chapter outlines two different methods of obtaining feedback on the appropriateness of the referrals that are provided. In addition, the issues related to updating the referral system are addressed.

In an attempt to track the progress of clients referred to a helping agency, we suggest the use of an interagency referral form. In this chapter we describe two different types of interagency referral forms: a multiple-copy interagency referral form used by several social service agencies in Lawrence, Kansas, and a single-copy interagency referral form used by social service agencies in Topeka, Kansas. Both types of referral forms serve the function of keeping the referral agency informed of the appropriateness and quality of its referrals. Your community might have a similar form that is currently used by social service agencies. If not, feel free to adopt either of the forms described here or to change the forms to meet the specific needs of your community.

A multiple-copy interagency referral form is one method of keeping track of client referrals. The form can provide a permanent record of referrals for the referring agency, the client, and the helping agency. In addition, one copy of the form might contain a request for the helping agency to provide feedback on whether the client kept the appointment and, if so, what services were provided. This information, if returned by mail to the referring agency, provides feedback on the appropriateness of the referral. More direct information on client satisfaction with services received might also be obtained by attaching a client satisfaction rating item to the client's copy of the referral form.

We have found that color coding the four copies of the referral form enables staff to discriminate what should be done with each copy on the basis of color. Thus, a white copy might be retained by the referring agency; a yellow copy might be retained by the helping agency; a blue copy might be retained by the client; and a gold copy might be used to provide feedback to the referring agency.

The forms, if printed on thin self-carboned paper and bound in sets of 50, are a convenient method of providing all of the information about a referral to all interested parties. At the same time, the information only needs to be written on the original top page of the form. The following pages contain samples of the four pages of the referral forms used by social service agencies in Lawrence, Kansas.

INTERAGENCY REFERRAL FORM

REFERRAL AGENCY COPY: Keep this copy for your own files.

Client's Name_____
Address_____
Phone_____

Referral Agency_____
Address_____
Phone_____
Referred by_____
Date_____

Agency Referred to_____
Address_____
Phone_____
Appointment with_____
Day of Week_____
Date_____
Time_____[ ] [ ]
                  a.m. p.m.

REASON FOR REFERRAL:_____
_____
_____

INTERAGENCY REFERRAL FORM

HELPING AGENCY COPY: This person has been referred to your facility for service. This copy is for your use.

Client's Name_____
Address_____
Phone_____

Referral Agency_____
Address_____
Phone_____
Referred by_____
Date_____

Agency Referred to_____
Address_____
Phone_____
Appointment with_____
Day of Week_____
Date_____
Time_____ | || |
a.m. p.m.

REASON FOR REFERRAL:_____
_____
_____

INTERAGENCY REFERRAL FORM

CLIENT'S COPY: This copy of the referral form is for you as a reminder of the time and location of your appointment. Please take this copy with you to your appointment. Thank you.

Client's Name_____
Address_____
Phone_____

Referred Agency_____
Address_____
Phone_____
Referred by_____
Date_____

Agency Referred to_____
Address_____
Phone_____
Appointment with_____
Day of Week_____
Date_____
Time_____ [ ] [ ]
a.m. p.m.

REASON FOR REFERRAL:_____
_____
_____

INTERAGENCY
REFERRAL FORM

FEEDBACK COPY: This person
has been referred to your facility for
service. Please complete this form
and return it to our office as soon as
possible after the appointment date.
This information will be used to
help improve our referrals. Thank you.

Client's name_____

Address_____

Phone_____

Referral Agency_____   Agency Referred to_____

Address_____   Address_____

Phone_____   Phone_____

Referred by_____   Appointment with_____

Date_____   Day of Week_____

                                        Date_____

                                        Time_____ [ ] [ ]
                                                  a.m. p.m.

REASON FOR REFERRAL:_____

_____

_____

Did the person keep the appointment? ____   ____
                                       yes   no

Was the referral appropriate?____   ____
                             yes   no

Services rendered:_____

_____

Signature:_____ Date:_____

We have found that some agencies do not return the feedback copy
without a reminder. Usually a call to the person at the helping
agency, with whom the appointment was made, results in obtaining
information about the outcome of the referral. If suitable rationales
for returning the feedback forms (e.g., so that future referrals will be
appropriate and to save time for the helping agency) are provided, the
helping agencies may be more likely to contribute the extra effort
required to return the feedback form.

If your agency is not able to receive the level of feedback that you
feel is necessary to justify mailing the multiple-copy referral form,
another option is to use a single-page form. The referral form on the

following page was developed in collaboration with the Community Resources Council (CRC) of Topeka. As you will note, this form includes prompts for the social service worker to note whether this is a telephone referral or a walk-in client, if transportation is needed by the client, if the client is eligible for the services, and the date the case should be followed up. In addition, the form provides space for the follow-up results and outcome of the referral. The bottom of the page can be completed as an appointment reminder for walk-in clients.

I&R INTERVIEW FORM   ☐ Telephone referral
                           ☐ Walk-in

Client's Name_____ Phone_____
Address_____ Zip_____
. . . .
Client's Problem/Need_____
_____
_____
_____

REFERRED TO (agency)_____ (person)_____
Agency Phone_____ Date of Referral_____
TRANSPORTATION NEEDED?   Yes   No
ELIGIBILITY REQUIREMENTS?   None Yes, client apparently
                                 qualified for service

TO BE FOLLOWED UP ON (date)_____

FOLLOW UP RESULTS
  Date Agency Contacted:_____
  Date Client Contacted:_____

OUTCOME OF THE REFERRAL
☐ Information only, no appointment made
☐ Referral made/service verified by follow up
☐ No show (contact client for reason; in mental health the referral
   agency is responsible for this)
☐ Misreferral (state reason_____)
☐ Service not available as listed (send Update Verification Request
   to CRC)
☐ Other (specify)_____
   _____

☐ Waiting List

. . . .
APPOINTMENT REMINDER

                    _____Time
                    _____Day of the Week
                    _____Month/Date
Person appointment is with_____
Agency_____ Address_____
Phone_____

The procedure involved in following-up a client referral is depicted in the flow chart. This follow-up procedure should be initiated whenever a copy of the interagency feedback form is returned or if one week beyond the client's appointment time passes without receiving any feedback. The follow-up procedure provides information about the appropriateness of the referral, whether the client kept the appointment, and whether the required services were rendered. If, for any reason, it appears that the needed services were not provided, it is important that the referral agent contact the client to determine if the problem has been solved. Similarly, spot check phone calls to clients regarding their satisfaction with the services received from the helping agency might also be conducted. The follow-up procedures help insure that the referral services were actually of assistance to clients.

Regardless of the type of feedback form you decide upon, the feedback can serve the function of keeping the social service directory up-to-date. Whenever you receive feedback about an agency indicating that the service was not rendered or the referral was inappropriate, then the directory problem-service cards should be revised accordingly. Similarly, when client satisfaction with an agency's service(s) is low, that agency might be temporarily deleted from the social service directory.

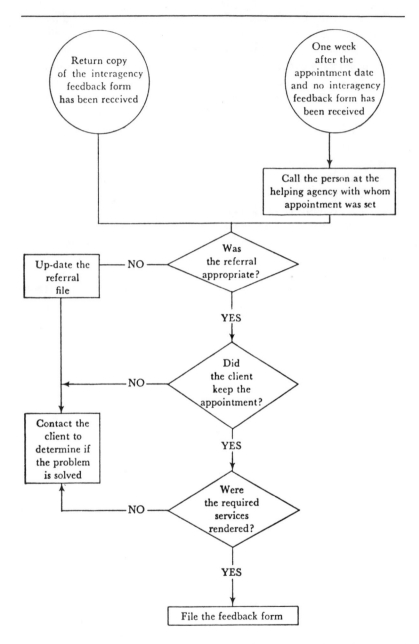

If more than one agency in the same community is using the information and referral system, one of the agencies might be willing to coordinate the process of updating. For example, in Topeka, the Community Resources Council has accepted the task of keeping the referral system up-to-date. The council has developed a form letter that any agency using the referral system can complete to request an update of the directory. This form is printed below. In this way, the system can be updated whenever there is a new agency in town, a program within an existing agency is changed, an agency goes out of existence, or there are administrative changes at an agency.

This information can be verified by the agency in charge of keeping the system up-to-date. Then, the information can be distributed to all of the social service agencies using the information and referral system. An organization with a monthly newsletter is an especially good candidate for the job of keeping the file up-to-date. A newsletter permits easy distribution to participating agencies at a minimal additional cost. In the absence of an existing community newsletter, the information might be printed as a public service in the local newspaper.

COMMUNITY RESOURCES FILE Request for Update

Date of Request ____/____/____
Person Making Request_____
Agency Making Request_____

TYPE OF CHANGE

    [ ] New Agency
    [ ] Program change within existing agency (program added,
       deleted, modified)
    [ ] Remove Agency from file
    [ ] New executive officer/phone/address/name change
How did you find out about this change? (newspaper, personal
contact, I & R)_____

_____
_____

Please attach any supporting documents (brochure, news
    clipping, correspondence)
Specify change (or indicate that this is detailed in the supporting
    documents)

_____
_____
_____

DO NOT WRITE BELOW THIS LINE

FOR CRC USE ONLY

Verified by_____

How was this verified?_____

_____
_____

DISPOSITION
    [ ] Error, no change indicated
    [ ] Hold, change not yet implemented
    [ ] Verified, disseminate update to all parties

Chapter 4

TRAINING COMMUNITY SERVICE WORKERS
IN REFERRAL SKILLS

Once you have developed the information and referral directory for your community and have decided on a procedure for promoting interagency feedback, it is important to train community service workers in how to use the referral system. Many program developers set up a program and let people use it as they will, with the expectation that everything will work out. However, in our experience, the presence of an information and referral directory and interagency referral forms is insufficient for producing effective referral services. We have found that during a pretraining condition, in which the directory and referral forms were made available, community service workers at one social service agency performed a low rate of the behaviors involved in using the directory, completing an interagency referral form, and arranging appointments for their clients. In addition, only 44% of the referrals provided by these untrained community service workers were to agencies that actually offered a service needed by the client. This low level of appropriate referrals was found with both new staff and experienced community service workers (Mathews and Fawcett, 1979b).

The second half of this book is designed to be used to teach information and referral skills to volunteer community workers, new staff members, and experienced helpers. Part II contains training lessons that may be used to teach these skills under the guidance of an instructor. We feel that by following the recommended teaching plan, instructors can successfully teach the referral skills.

OVERVIEW OF THE TEACHING OBJECTIVES

Without information and referral skills, it may be difficult for social service workers to refer clients to an agency where they can receive the help needed. Accordingly, the teaching objectives include the skills of using the social service directory, completing an interagency referral form, arranging an appointment for a client, and handling special problem referrals.

OVERVIEW OF THE TRAINING METHOD

The goal of this behaviorally based training method is to teach community service workers to perform the skills involved in providing a referral. The goal is an improvement in actual behavior, rather than merely a change in attitude or an increase in knowledge. Accordingly, modeling or demonstrating the skill, precise descriptions of what is involved in the skills, and practice and feedback on performance are all important elements of the teaching method.

The training method has been devised so that each referral skill has been analyzed in terms of individual behaviors to be learned. Each training lesson contains information about a particular skill, such as how to use the social service directory. After this information is learned, it is put to use by practice in role-playing situations. The skill is mastered through practice of the skill and feedback on performance. Mastery of one skill is required before study is begun on the next skill.

Each skill is taught in a separate training lesson. A lesson consists of the following five parts:

(1) *instructions* that include a rationale for describing the importance of each skill and information explaining why, when, and how to do each aspect of the particular referral skill
(2) a *summary* section in which the critical points of the lesson are outlined
(3) a *study guide* that consists of questions by which the learner's knowledge of the instructions may be tested
(4) *role-playing practice situations* that provide the student with an opportunity to practice the behaviors and receive corrective feedback
(5) a *quality check* that provides the student with an opportunity to demonstrate the learned activities.

Although the training lessons are quite comprehensive, successful learning of the referral skills is enhanced by the skillful hand of a trainer or instructor. Though a variety of methods might be used to teach these objectives successfully, our research suggests the particular importance of several teaching activities. Specifically, we recommend providing:

(1) a rationale for the importance of each skill
(2) a demonstration of each skill
(3) instruction in when and how to use the skill
(4) an opportunity to practice the behavior
(5) constructive feedback on performance during practice
(6) an evaluation of the level of the learning.

THE SPECIFIC TRAINING METHOD

Briefly then, the training method goes as follows: The instructor begins with a rationale stating why the skill is important. The instructor then demonstrates or models the referral skill that is to be trained. To model the skill, the instructor plays the part of the helper and an assistant plays the part of a client. In this way, the instructor acts out the skills involved in providing a referral. Alternatively, the instructor may read or describe a referral situation, such as those described in the complete examples found in each training lesson.

We suggest that the instructor perform a number of teaching activities to provide instruction in when and how to use each particular referral skill. First, the instructor assigns the instructions section for the relevant training lesson. Second, the student completes the study guide questions to demonstrate an understanding of the written material. Students' answers may be scored using the study guide answer key that follows each quiz. Third, it is useful to review with the student the description of the individual behaviors involved in each skill, rationales for these behaviors, and examples of the behaviors. Fourth, the instructor may then redemonstrate the referral skill and review the rationale for the skill and the description of when to use the skill. After the student has learned *about* the skill, it is time to practice *how* to use it.

The practice situations consist of an opportunity to practice the behaviors involved in the skill, followed by corrective feedback on performance from the instructor or student partner. Several hypothetical referral situations are included at the end of each lesson. The instructor or a student partner can play the role of a client as the student tries to apply the newly acquired skill to the particular situation. The partner may also use the behavioral checklist during role-playing to record whether the identified activities were actually performed. Accordingly, the checklist will help the partner provide constructive feedback. Of course, these practice situations should be repeated until the student can perform the skill perfectly. (Note: Depending upon the instructor's preference, the role-playing partner of the student may be another community service worker, a friend, or the instructor.)

The final step is the quality check. This is the final check to evaluate whether the student has learned the skill. It is recommended that these role-playing sessions be conducted by an instructor or teaching assistant, not a student partner. Accordingly, scripts and checklists for these role-playing sessions are also provided in the appendix. Upon demonstration of the skill to the instructor's satisfaction, the student may begin learning the next referral skill. Unsatisfactory performance should be followed by further practice, feedback, and a new quality check situation. The same training procedure should be followed for each of the referral skills. Since the skills build on each other, the student should not begin training in a new skill until competence has been demonstrated with the previous one. More detail on how to implement the training method is provided in the remaining sections of this chapter.

STATING RATIONALES

We encourage you to highlight for students *why* they are learning these particular referral skills. In giving a rationale for using a skill, it is helpful to remember to talk about what benefits are to be gained by the helper or the client and what problems are to be avoided by the helper or the client through this activity. Benefits, such as helping the client solve a problem, should be included. Or, the avoidance or problems, such as avoiding sending clients on a dead-end referral, might be mentioned.

Many rationales contain the words *because* or *is designed to*. Here is a rationale for the referral skill of completing an interagency referral form that describes the benefits to be gained by using this skill:

> By completing an interagency referral form, you will provide a record of the referrals provided by your agency, provide an appointment

reminder for your client, and provide a prompt to check up on the client's success in solving the problem.

A strong rationale helps highlight the importance of the skill. This will increase the likelihood that the learned skills will be used after the completion of training.

DEMONSTRATING THE REFERRAL SKILL

It is recommended that the instructor demonstrate or model the complete referral skill before the student is asked to do any reading. Of course, the demonstration may be by a teaching assistant or instructor and may be to one or more students at a time. The demonstration should be repeated when the students have completed the instructions section of the training lesson.

A good model or demonstration involves several elements. First, the model should include a *complete* and *accurate* demonstration of the behaviors involved in the skill. (It is not sufficient to describe what should be done; rather, show *how* it is done for a particular referral situation.) This might consist of playing the part of a social service worker with a student who has been advised how to play the part of a client. Alternatively, the instructor might read or paraphrase the complete example provided at the end of the chapter.

If the model is incomplete, inaccurate, or different from what is described in the instructions, it will serve to confuse rather than instruct the students. After demonstrating the skill, the instructor should point out what was important in the model and how each aspect of the model meets the criterion defined in the instructions. After this discussion it is a good idea to model the skill once again so that students may review the skill as it should be performed.

ASSIGNING THE INSTRUCTIONS SECTION

When assigning the instructions section, we recommend that you ask students to study only one training lesson at a time. You may find it helpful to ask the student to make a written answer to the study guide questions before beginning the practice sessions. To check this, some instructors and teaching assistants find it useful to give brief oral or written quizzes to students before beginning the role-playing practice sessions. Answer keys for the study questions are provided immediately following the quiz. When reviewing the instructions section, the instructor might invite students to share their questions about when, why, and how to use the skill.

GIVING EXAMPLES OF REFERRAL SKILLS

Examples give the student an idea of the different kinds of situations that call for the use of the referral activities and the variety of acceptable forms that a skill may take. Some examples of referral skills and situations are provided in the training lessons. As with demonstrating a skill, it is critical that your examples are consistent with the instructions. The more varied your examples and the closer they are to reality, the greater the likelihood that students will be able to apply their learning to actual helping situations.

SETTING UP PRACTICE SESSIONS

Role-playing situations and instructions for their use during practice sessions are provided at the end of each training lesson. The practice sessions are designed to provide an opportunity for each student to practice a referral skill and receive corrective feedback. By putting the skills to use, students can prepare for similar roles with actual clients.

Role-playing may require some explanation for the students. In role-playing, the student acts as a helper with a person playing the role of a client in need of help. (Note: At the discretion of the instructor, the student's partner may be another student, a teaching assistant, or the instructor. If students serve as partners for each other, we encourage you to avoid pairing friends with each other as this may make it more difficult for them to take the role-playing situations seriously.) To role-play the part of a client, the partner first reads the description of the problem situation (or makes up a new situation if preferred). These practice situations should continue until the student and partner feel that the skill has been mastered. We recommend that role-playing practice continue until the student has performed all of the referral behaviors perfectly in at least two consecutive practice situations.

If additional practice situations are needed, the instructor, teaching assistant, or students may make up their own situations and script lines using the available situations as examples.

Constructive feedback on performance in these practice situations may be provided by another student, a teaching assistant, or the instructor. Constructive feedback is specific, describing the positive aspects of performance as well as the aspects needing improvement. The student's partner should restrict comments to observable behavior, avoiding value judgments or criticisms of the student. You may wish to remind partners to focus on improving the referral behaviors of the students and avoid harsh criticisms of the student's genuine efforts to learn.

We have found that a good way to encourage constructive feedback during practice sessions is to use the practice checklists. The checklists, included at the end of each lesson, consist of tally sheets on which the partner notes what is done well and what might be improved.

We recommend that you and your assistants give feedback in the following way:

(1) Describe to the student the activities listed on the checklist that were done correctly.
(2) Describe the activities that were either omitted or done incorrectly.
(3) If necessary, describe how these activities could be done correctly.
(4) Ask the student to practice each of the activities performed incorrectly.
(5) Encourage the student to ask questions about anything that is confusing.
(6) Practice that segment again with the student.

Role-playing partners should be very specific about what the student did incorrectly. For example, while practicing the skills involved in arranging an appointment for a client, if the student called the agency and described the client's problem, without ever stating who she/he was and where she/he worked, constructive feedback might involved saying: "You did call the agency and describe the client's problem. However, you forgot to give your name and affiliation." This specific feedback would be better than a general comment of, "You did not do it right," because the former describes exactly what was done right and what was done incorrectly.

SETTING UP THE QUALITY CHECKS

The quality checks are designed to assess the performance of the trainee in new role-playing situations. Be certain to use role-playing situations never before seen by the student so that practice may not account for improvements. New role-playing situations for the quality checks are provided in the appendix.

As with the practice situations, referral situations are provided for the students. We recommend that either a teaching assistant or the instructor serve as evaluator for the quality checks. This will give the instructor an opportunity to evaluate the progress of students in acquiring referral skills. The quality checklist may be used to identify strengths and/or weaknesses and to help determine whether further training is required. Though the final judgment of whether the skill has been learned rests with the instructor, we recommend that students demonstrate perfect performance for at least one role-playing session before being assigned the instructions for the next referral skill.

PROVIDING FOLLOW-UP CONSULTATION

Though training may be "officially" over, the instructor retains some responsibility for supervising the student's subsequent use of these referral skills. In the weeks immediately following training, ask the students to inform you of their use of these skills and any problems or successes that may have occurred. Be certain that experienced social service workers or counselors are available to provide back-up consultation and advice. Basic ethical practice demands attention to these safeguards for the clients' welfare. Following is a summary of steps in the entire teaching plan:

(1) introduce the training methods to students
(2) demonstrate the complete set of skills
(3) repeat this training sequence for each training lesson
    (a) provide a rationale for the skill
    (b) demonstrate the specific skill
    (c) assign the instructions
    (d) give feedback on the study guide
    (e) review the content of the instructions and answer questions
    (f) redemonstrate the skill
    (g) provide an opportunity to practice the skill in role-playing situations
    (h) provide corrective feedback
    (i) practice until the skill is mastered
    (j) provide a quality check by evaluating performance in a new situation
    (k) repractice and provide additional quality checks as necessary
(4) provide follow-up consultation after training while the students are providing referrals.

Part II

PROVIDING INFORMATION AND
REFERRAL SERVICES

WHAT IS INVOLVED IN PROVIDING REFERRALS?

In many communities, the complex activity of providing information and referral is reserved for only the most experienced social service agency personnel. Through years of experience, these "super service-givers" have formulated their own informal social service directories. Methods for providing referrals and scheduling client appointments have evolved in a similar fashion—through trial and error. As a result, there are often as many different ideas about where and how to obtain needed help for a client as their are experienced service-givers. This lack of specification makes it virtually impossible to share referral skills with other potential helpers.

A second major goal of this book is to provide an opportunity for systematic training in information and referral skills. The book is designed to accompany an information and referral directory developed for your own community. The directory contains an index which lists possible problem categories (e.g., transportation), a listing of problems and services that provides detailed information about each service offered in the community, and a listing of all of the known social service agencies in the community. A set of interagency referral forms can be used to obtain follow-up information on the appropriateness of referrals and the services that your clients receive. Thus, the complete information and referral system consists of training materials for service-givers, a social service directory, and interagency referral forms.

The remainder of this book contains a series of training lessons designed to teach the skills associated with providing information and referral. Each lesson consists of written instructions, study guides, and opportunities to practice the referral behaviors and receive feedback. Participation in this training requires a minimum of reading and writing skills at approximately the fifth-grade level. As such, the program may be well-suited for use by nonprofessional helpers, volunteers, and other community service workers.

The training materials contained in the book are designed to teach the skills required to use an information and referral directory, to complete interagency referral forms, and to arrange client appointments. Each lesson teaches one of these skills. However, before you begin the first training lesson, it might be useful to get a better idea of what is involved in providing a referral. The flow chart below displays the procedure used in referring a client to another agency. The referral agent first matches the client's problem to an index listing in the social service directory. The appropriate problem-service card in the directory is then checked to determine if the service provided is appropriate to the client's problem. If appropriate, the helping agency is then called and an appointment is arranged for the client. In addition, an interagency referral form is completed and copies are given to the client and the helping agency, and one copy is retained by the referral agency. While your particular agency may choose to modify this procedure, the basic components have proven appropriate for several agencies that have adopted this referral system.

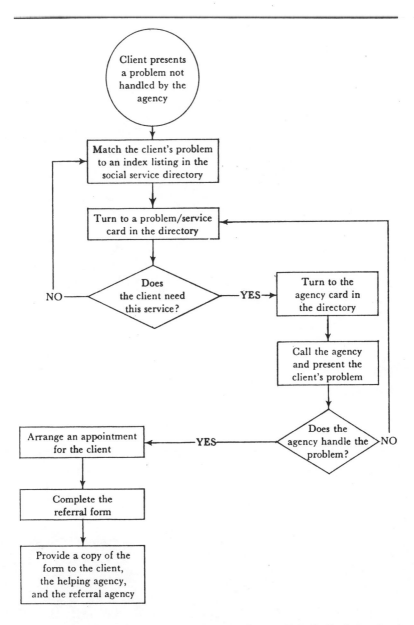

Chapter 5

USING THE SOCIAL SERVICE DIRECTORY

This chapter describes a procedure for using the social service directory prepared for your local community. The directory consists of three sections: (1) an index that lists possible problem categories (e.g., transportation); (2) problem-service cards that provide information about each service offered in the community; and (3) a directory of social service agencies within the community.

The social service directory is designed to help community service workers select the appropriate agency for client referrals. Using the directory will enable staff members to provide appropriate referrals without memorizing all of the services available in the community.

Of course, to be able to use the social service directory, the staff member must first determine the client's problems. Since clients rarely have only one problem, the staff member should determine each problem and look up each problem separately.

It is all too often the case that clients in need of help are sent from agency to agency without ever receiving the direct service that they require. This is a time-consuming and frustrating experience for a person in need of help. It is also true that many agency staff members are not quite sure what to do when a client requires a service that is not offered by their agency. This, too, can be a frustrating and time-consuming experience for the agency staff. Effective use of the social service directory for your community will help to simplify the task of providing quick, appropriate referrals for clients who require a service that is not offered by your agency. You should perform the activities involved in using the social service directory whenever a client requires a service that is not provided by your agency.

To use the social service directory, you will need to have on hand: a social service directory, a sheet of scratch paper, and a pencil. We recommend seven activities to use the social service directory: match the client's problem to an index listing; write possible problem-service listings; turn to the problem-service card; and determine if the service meets the client's needs. If the service *does* meet the client's needs, you should write the agency name on scratch paper and determine the client's eligibility. This is merely an overview of the steps involved in using the directory. Each activity is described in detail below.

MATCH THE CLIENT'S PROBLEM TO AN INDEX LISTING

After you have asked the client what the problem is, we suggest that you look through the index cards for the client's problem. The index lists all of the problem and service categories that are contained in the social service directory. Matching the client's problem to an index listing sometimes requires looking at a number of categories. For example, if Mrs. Smith comes to the center with the problem of needing new reading glasses, you might look in the index under the categories Financial Assistance and Medical. Of course, you would not look under categories such as Child Care or Yard Work. If Mrs. Smith's vision was so poor that she could not work without her glasses, you might look under Emergency Assistance or Blind. Consider also the example of a client who says that his two-year-old son has something wrong with him because he never responds when people talk to him. As a staff member, you might look in the index under Medical, Hearing (Children), Hearing (Evaluation), Hearing (Problems), or Mental Health. Because the client's child is not having trouble talking, just hearing, you would not look under Speech. Matching the client's problem to an index listing will enable you to locate the problem-service categories that are best suited to the client's needs.

WRITE ALL POSSIBLE LISTINGS ON SCRATCH PAPER

As you are looking through the index, we recommend that you write each potentially appropriate problem or service category (from the index) on a sheet of scratch paper. You should write each category exactly as it appears in the index. If, however, the index listing cross-lists another service [e.g., EMOTIONAL PROBLEMS (see MENTAL HEALTH)], you should write the primary entry (e.g., MENTAL HEALTH) on the scratch paper. For example, for Mrs. Smith's problem of needing glasses, you would list Financial Assistance and Medical. You might also list Elderly, Emergency Assistance, or Blind, if any of those categories was appropriate for Mrs. Smith's situation. For the boy with the hearing problem, you would list Medical, Hearing (Children), Hearing (Evaluation), Hearing (Problems), and Mental Health.

Listing all possibly appropriate categories will help you avoid having to refer back to the index later. It is important to write each category exactly as it appears in the primary entry of the index because that is how that category is listed throughout the social service directory. The cross-listings are provided for your convenience in matching the client's problem to an index listing. If you write the category as it appears in the primary entry of the index, it will be much easier to find the listing in problem-service section of the directory.

TURN TO THE PROBLEM-SERVICE CARD

After you have noted each possible category, you should find the problem-service card that matches the first category on your sheet of paper. The problem-service cards are located after the index and are filed in alphabetical order. There is at least one problem-service card for each primary index entry. For example, if the first listing on the scratch paper is Financial Assistance, you would first turn to the problem-service cards filed under F. Financial Assistance would be found before Food, but after Federal Programs. Similarly, Counseling (Budget) could be found under the C listings before Counseling (Child Abuse) and after Complaints. Turning to the problem-service card will enable you to find out more about the service that is offered and the specific problems handled by a local agency.

DETERMINE IF THE SERVICE MEETS THE CLIENT'S NEEDS

Next, you should read the description of the problem handled and decide if it is the same as the client's problem. The "problem handled" descriptions are very specific and should indicate whether the service offered will meet your client's needs. Consider the problem-service card with the heading Elderly (Transportation) with this description: "Problem handled: transportation to any location in town. Participants picked up and delivered to door." If your client is an elderly woman who needs to go to a doctor in town, this service is probably the one that is needed. However, if your client is an elderly woman who needs to go to a doctor in another city, this service would not be appropriate because it specifies "any location *in town.*" Another example is the listing of Blind (Services for) with this description: "Any blind person may obtain a free receiver which picks up special broadcasts of news and programs where people read books aloud." This service is appropriate if your client is a person who wants to hear news broadcasts, but it is not appropriate if your client is a blind person who needs to go to the store for groceries. Determining if the service offered will meet the client's needs will help you insure that you are helping the client with his or her actual problem—a radio receiver will not get a blind person to the grocery store!

If the service listed on the problem-service card *is not* what the client needs, turn to the next problem-service card on your list and determine if that service will meet the client's needs. Repeat this process until a service is located that will meet the client's needs. If the service listed on the problem-service card *is* what the client needs, then go on to the next activities in this chapter.

WRITE THE AGENCY NAME

After you have found a problem-service card that matches the client's problems, write on scratch paper the names of all agencies that offer the needed service. The agency name is written on the card beside the word *Contact.* Sometimes there will be a person's name written beside the agency name. If this is the case, you should also write that person's name on your scratch paper. Below is an example of a problem service card with several agencies listed:

COUNSELING (Budget)

Problem handled: Budget counseling and money management assist-
                   ance available to anyone.
Contact: 10th Street Mental Health Center
Contact: Legal Aid Society (Jason McHenry)

In this example, you would write "10th Street Mental Health Center" and "Legal Aid Society (Jason McHenry)" on a sheet of scratch paper. It is important to write the names of all appropriate agencies to avoid having to return to the problem-service card if one agency cannot provide the needed service. You should write the name of the contact *person* as well as the agency because it is this person who handles that specific service for the agency.

DETERMINE CLIENT'S ELIGIBILITY

Next, you should turn to the agency card for the first agency listed on your scratch paper. The agency cards are arranged in alphabetical order and are located behind the problem-service cards. When you have found the appropriate agency card, read the eligibility requirements that are listed beside Eligibility. Some examples of eligibility requirements include a specific income, age, disability, and so on. Next, you should decide whether your client meets the requirements of the agency. That is, "Is she/he eligible to receive the services?" It may be necessary to ask the client specific questions to determine if she/he meets the requirements of the agency. For example, the service described on the problem-service card might be a perfect match for Bill Brown's problem, but to be eligible for the service the client must be over 62. If Bill is only 57 years old, it would be inappropriate to refer him to that agency. However, a client earning only $3,400 per year would be quite eligible for services from an agency that requires an annual income of less than $3,600. Checking the client's eligibility for the agency's services will help insure that your client will be able to receive the needed services upon arriving at the agency. You will not waste your clients' time by referring them to agencies that cannot provide the needed services because of eligibility problems.

To provide a better understanding of how the steps involved in using the social service directory fit together, we have provided a narrative. In this example, Dr. Paul Marlowe is working as a psychologist for the East Boston Community Mental Health Center. During a counseling session with Mrs. Ban, he found that one of her most current, pressing problems was that the power company had cut off her electricity for failure to pay her power bill. Mrs. Ban currently had no means of paying the bill and had an infant to care for in her home. Therefore, Dr. Marlowe decided to use the social service directory to locate an agency that would be able to help her with this problem. While checking the directory's index, Dr. Marlowe found several listings that might help with Mrs. Ban's problem. These included: Budget Counseling, Employment Counseling, Economic Assistance, and Utility Assistance. After writing down each of these listings, he decided to check the problem-service card for Economic Assistance. The program he found described under the heading of Economic Assistance read: "Supplemental income for persons over 65 years of age or with a physical disability." Because this program did not meet Mrs. Ban's needs, he turned to the card for Utility Assistance. This card read: "Emergency assistance for utility turnoff notices when the person cannot afford to pay." He decided that this service was a perfect match for her needs, so he wrote the name of the agency (Brook Hollow Center) on a sheet of scratch paper and turned to Brook Hollow Center's agency card in the back of the directory. The only eligibility requirement for the service was financial need. Mrs. Ban certainly seemed to meet this requirement. Thus, he had used the social service directory to locate assistance from an appropriate agency.

In summary, the steps that we have found helpful in using the social service directory include:

(1) match the client's problem to an index listing
(2) write all possible listings on scratch paper
(3) turn to the problem-service card
(4) determine if the service meets the client's needs.

If the service *does* meet the client's needs:

(5) write the agency name
(6) determine the client's eligibility.

STUDY GUIDE:
USING THE SOCIAL SERVICE DIRECTORY

1. What types of information are contained in the social service directory?

2. What problems can be avoided by using the social service directory?

3. Describe the activities involved in using the social service directory.

4. Describe the importance of matching the service to the client's needs.

STUDY GUIDE ANSWER KEY:
USING THE SOCIAL SERVICE DIRECTORY

1. The three types of information contained in the social service directory include:
    (a) an index of services offered
    (b) detailed descriptions of each of the problems handled
    (c) descriptions of each of the local agencies offering each service.
2. By using the social service directory you can avoid such problems as:
    (a) sending a client to an inappropriate agency
    (b) not knowing how to help a client
    (c) spending a great deal of the client's time trying to find an agency that can help.
3. The activities involved in using the social service directory include:
    (a) match the client's problem to an index listing
    (b) write all possible listings on scratch paper
    (c) turn to the problem-service card
    (d) determine if the service meets the client's needs
    (e) write the agency name
    (f) determine the client's eligibility.
4. If you provide a referral for a client to an agency that offers a service that is different than the client's problem, you run the risk of not helping the client with the problem that was presented.

SITUATIONAL EXAMPLE:
USING THE SOCIAL SERVICE DIRECTORY

Fill in the blank with an example that applies each rule learned in this lesson to the situation, checking your answer after each question. An answer key is provided immediately following the situational examples.

Situation: You are working in the office at Westside Center when you get a telephone call from Mrs. Becker. She tells you that she is 89 years old and has just gotten out of the hospital where she had an operation. Because she is so weak, she is not able to keep up the housework. She also tells you that her doctor said that she will be healthy enough to go out and dig the potatoes from her garden within two or three weeks.

1. Match the client's problem to an index listing. Write all appropriate index listings on scratch paper.

Index

Birth Control
Blind
Child Care
Clothing
Counseling
 –Crisis
 –Religious
 –Welfare

Education
 –Adult Basic
 –Living Skills
 –Homemaking
 –Tutoring
Elderly
 –Companionship
 –Housecleaning
 –Housing
 –Transportation

Emergency Assistance
 –Food
 –Medical
Financial Assistance
Home Improvement Repairs
Legal Problems
Mentally Retarded

List any appropriate index listing(s):_____

Turn to the problem service card:

ELDERLY (Housecleaning)

Problem Handled: Provides someone to help with housecleaning on a temporary basis.

Contact: Visiting Nurses Association

---

2. Determine if the service offered is what the client needs.
Is this a service the client needs?_____
3. Write the agency name on scratch paper.

---

4. Turn to the agency card and write the agency's phone number on scratch paper.

VISITING NURSES ASSOCIATION

Address: 701 New Hampshire
Phone: 843-3738
Hours: 8:30-5:00, M-F
Eligibility: patients must be housebound, need referral from a local agency or doctor
Appointments Accepted: Yes—required

Phone Number:_____
5. Determine the client's eligibility.
Is Mrs. Becker eligible?_____

SITUATIONAL EXAMPLE ANSWER KEY: USING THE SOCIAL SERVICE DIRECTORY

1. *Match and write index listings.*
   Elderly—Housecleaning
2. *Determine if this is a needed service.*
   Yes
3. *Write the agency name.*
   Visiting Nurses Association
4. *Write agency phone number.*
   843-3738
5. *Determine eligibility.*
   Yes

SITUATIONS TO PRACTICE USING THE
SOCIAL SERVICE DIRECTORY

We have found that it is helpful to put into practice immediately the new skills that you have learned. Thus, we have included this section of the lesson to help you practice the skill of using the social service directory.

To practice this skill will require a social service directory for your community. Below are several referral situations that might occur. For each situation, assume that your agency does not offer the needed service. Use the directory developed for your community to select the appropriate organizations to handle each client situation.

A teenager comes to you with a description of a family situation. His father has a drinking problem and beats his mother and younger brother. He is unwilling to go to the police, or have them called in, but wants help for his mother and brother.

A woman with three young children has come to you for help in paying this month's rent. Her husband has just left her and she has no job skills.

A man has come to you because he purchased a used refrigerator which, once delivered, did not work. He did not receive a written guarantee, but had been promised that the refrigerator would work. Now the seller refuses to stand behind his word.

A woman comes to your agency because she is worried about her three-year-old daughter. The little girl seems to be developing normally, except that she has not learned to talk.

A man with five dependents has just been laid off work. He has applied for unemployment, but must wait four days to receive an unemployment check. His immediate problem is that his family has no food for the next few days.

An elderly man calls you for help. He was just released from the hospital and requires a special diet. However, he is not physically able to prepare his own meals. He lives alone and does not know what to do.

CHECKLIST: USING THE SOCIAL SERVICE DIRECTORY

1. Match the client's problem to an index listing.
2. Write all possible listings on scratch paper.
3. Turn to the problem-service card.
4. Determine if the service meets the need.
5. Determine the client's eligibility.

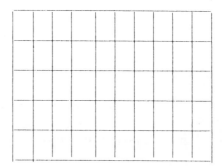

Chapter 6

ARRANGING AN APPOINTMENT FOR A CLIENT

Nothing is more frustrating than to have a serious problem and be sent from one agency to the next, without ever receiving any real help. This is an experience that all too many people have in common. One way that you, as a service giver, can reduce the chances of your clients bouncing from one agency to the next is to arrange an appointment for the client as part of the referral. Arranging an appointment insures that the desired service is still offered by the agency to which you plan to refer the client; it insures that someone will be available to help the client upon arrival; and it insures that the agency will be expecting the client. Accordingly, by arranging an appointment for every client, as a part of the referral, you will help your clients obtain the desired service with a minimum of hassle.

Once you have used the social service directory to identify an agency that offers the services that are needed by your client, we recommend that you call the agency and schedule an appointment for the client. We have found the following steps to be an effective method of arranging an appointment: call the agency; state your name and affiliation; state the client's problem; request help from the agency; request an appointment time; ask the client if the time is convenient; and thank the person.

CALL THE AGENCY

After you have identified an agency that appears to be able to help the client, we suggest that you call the agency on the telephone. The agency's telephone number is listed on the agency card located in the social service directory.

STATE NAME AND AFFILIATION

We recommend that you tell the person at the helping agency your name and the name of the organization for which you work. Examples of stating one's name and affiliation would include:

(1) "I'm Jim Meyer from the County Health Department."
(2) "Good morning, my name is Sue Estes. I'm with the Office on Aging."

This explanation lets the person you are calling know who he/she is speaking to and what agency you represent.

STATE THE CLIENT'S PROBLEM

We suggest that you explain that you have a client in need of assistance and state exactly what service is needed. This explanation should be accurate, yet brief. Do not mention the client's name. Below are examples of explanations of client problems:

(1) "I'm trying to find help for a client. She needs money for a medical prescription."
(2) "I have a client who needs to have his utility services restored."

This explanation lets the person know what the problem is. In this way the person can either help you with the problem or transfer you to someone at the agency who will be able to help. Many times the first person that you reach at an agency is not the person who can help with the problem. For that reason, in the interest of confidentiality, we recommend that your description of the problem be brief, with no mention of the client's name.

REQUEST HELP FROM THE AGENCY

It is important to ask if the agency can assist the client in the solution of the problem. Methods of requesting help include:

(1) "Can you help our client with her problem?"
(2) "Will your agency provide assistance for this person?"

This information will clarify whether the agency can provide the service needed by the client. Whenever an agency *cannot* help the client, thank the person and close the conversation. Return to the social service directory and call the next prospective agency until you find an agency that *can* help the client. Whenever the agency can help the client, follow the steps listed below.

REQUEST AN APPOINTMENT

We recommend that you ask the person at the agency to schedule an appointment for the client. This appointment should be for a specific time, on a specific day, and with a specific person. Below are examples of requests for appointments:

(1) "Could you set up an appointment for the client?"
(2) "Can we schedule an appointment with someone at your agency to help the client?"

An appointment will insure that someone at the agency expects the client and has taken responsibility for helping the client. Further, the client will know when to go to the agency and who to talk to upon arrival.

ASK THE CLIENT IF THE APPOINTMENT TIME IS CONVENIENT

You should ask the client if the appointment time is suitable. If the client is unable to go to the agency at the scheduled time, then arrange for another appointment time. It is usually possible to check with the client to see if the appointment time will work while you are on the phone with the helping agency. Examples of how to ask a client about the appointment time include:

(1) "Will you be able to go to the Vocational Rehabilitation Office this afternoon at 3:30?"
(2) "Is Thursday at 10:15 a.m. all right?"

Asking the client if the appointment time is convenient insures that the arranged time will work for both the client and the helping agency. It also increases the chances that the client will actually go to the agency to receive the needed services.

THANK THE PERSON

We recommend that you close the conversation by expressing your appreciation for the assistance that you have received. Below are examples of thanking a person:

(1) "Thanks a lot for your help."
(2) "Thanks, your assistance has been useful."

In situations in which the agency was not able to help the client, appropriate responses would include:

(1) "Well, thanks anyway. I appreciate your time."
(2) "Thank you for your time and for trying to help."

Thanking the person indicates your appreciation for the time and effort provided. Further, it may help strengthen relations between your agency and the agencies to which you provide referrals.

A narrative of what it might sound like for a service-giver to arrange an appointment for a client is provided below. In this example, Dr. Marlowe is arranging an appointment at Brook Hollow Center for Mrs. Ban for assistance with her utility bills. Dr. Marlowe dialed the telephone number listed for Brook Hollow Center on the agency card provided in the social service directory:

Brook Hollow: "Good morning, Brook Hollow Center. May I help you?"

Dr. Marlowe: "Yes. This is Paul Marlowe from the East Boston Community Mental Health Center. I have a client whose power has been cut off, and she can't afford to pay the bill to have it turned on. I was wondering if you might be able to help."

Brook Hollow: "Yes, we have some money left in this month's budget to use for utility cut-offs."

Dr. Marlowe: "Can we set up an appointment for the client?"

Brook Hollow: "Okay, I'll put her down for 4:30 this afternoon."

Dr. Marlowe: (To Mrs. Ban) "Is 4:30 this afternoon all right?"

Mrs. Ban: "Sure."

Dr. Marlowe: "Yes, 4:30 will be fine. Who should she ask for once she gets there?"

Brook Hollow: "The appointment is with Alice Phillip."

Dr. Marlowe: "Okay. Thank you so much for your help."
Brook Hollow: "You're welcome, good-bye."

To summarize, the following steps are recommended for scheduling an appointment for a client to receive services from another agency:

(1) call the agency
(2) state name and affiliation
(3) state the client's problem
(4) request help from the agency.

If the agency can help:

(5) request an appointment time
(6) ask the client if the appointment time is convenient
(7) thank the person.

STUDY GUIDE:
ARRANGING AN APPOINTMENT FOR A CLIENT

1. Why would you want to arrange an appointment for a client?

2. When should you arrange an appointment for the client?

3. Describe the activities involved in arranging a client appointment.

4. Why is it important to find out the name of the person that the appointment is with?

STUDY GUIDE ANSWER KEY:
ARRANGING AN APPOINTMENT FOR A CLIENT

1. By arranging an appointment for the client, you guarantee that the desired service is offered by the agency to which you refer the client, that there will be someone available to help the client, and that the client will be expected.
2. You should arrange an appointment for the client as a part of the referral, before the client leaves your agency.
3. The activities involved in arranging a client appointment include:
    (a) call the agency
    (b) state your name and affiliation
    (c) state the client's problem
    (d) request help from the agency
    (e) request an appointment time
    (f) ask the client if the appointment time is convenient
    (g) thank the person.
4. By scheduling an appointment with a *specific* person at the agency, the client knows who to ask for and you know who to contact to follow-up the referral.

SITUATIONAL EXAMPLE:
ARRANGING AN APPOINTMENT FOR A CLIENT

Fill in the blanks with a description of the activity that should be performed for the particular situation. Use the answer key to check your answer after each question.

Situation: John Green contacted the El Sol Center and asked for help since he and his family were being evicted. They did not have enough money for rent. Assume that you are the staff member at El Sol. By checking in the social service directory, you found that the agency that can handle John's problem is East Wind Center at 819 Sunny Side Drive, 669-8823.

1. Call the agency_____

2. State name and affiliation_____

3. State the client's problem_____

4. Request help from agency_____

The person at East Wind says, "Yes, we can help."

5. Request an appointment_____

The person at East Wind says, "Monday, April 11, at 10:00 a.m."

6. Ask the client if the time is convenient_____

John Green says, "Yes."

7. Request the name of the person that the appointment is with____

8. Thank the person_____

SITUATIONAL EXAMPLE ANSWER KEY: ARRANGING AN APPOINTMENT FOR A CLIENT

1. *Call the agency.*
   Sample answer: "Dial 669-8823"
2. *State name and affiliation*
   Sample answer: "Hello, I am *(student's name)* from El Sol."
3. *State client's problem.*
   Sample answer: "I have a client who is going to be evicted from his house because he didn't have enough money for rent."
4. *Request help from agency.*
   Sample answer: "Can your agency help our client?"
5. *Request an appointment time.*
   Sample answer: "Can you make an appointment for the client?"
6. *Ask the client if time is convenient.*
   Sample answer: "Will Monday, April 11 at 10:00 be all right?"
7. *Request the name of the person that the appointment is with.*
   Sample answer: "What is the name of the person that the appointment is with?"
8. *Thank the person.*
   Sample answer: "Thank you for your help."

SITUATIONS TO PRACTICE ARRANGING AN APPOINTMENT FOR A CLIENT

Six situations are provided for you to practice arranging client appointments. To practice each situation, you will need a partner to help you. This partner can be a coworker, a member of your family, a friend, or the person who developed the information and referral system for your community.

Your partner will play the part of the person that you call to arrange an appointment for the client. The partner will also play the part of the client. You should act as if you were actually arranging an appointment. (Do not simply state what you *would* do, rather, actually say or do it.) We have included six practice situations. If you wish, you may also create your own practice situations.

To practice the situation, the partner should read the description of the situation to you. Then, without looking at the script or book, you should use the skills described in this lesson to arrange the appointment for the client.

We recommend that the partner act as if this were a real situation for which he or she is really working at the social service organization that you call. This will give you a chance to practice telephoning people to schedule appointments for your clients. It would also be helpful if your partner would vary his or her responses to your questions regarding whether the agency can help your client and whether you can schedule an appointment for your client. This will give you practice dealing with a variety of responses from agencies.

We suggest that the partner use the checklist that follows the list of situations to give you feedback on your performance. Once you have both finished acting out the situation, the partner can check off all of the referral behaviors that you completed correctly. The partner should also note those behaviors that you did not do and those that you performed incorrectly. Using the checklist to guide the feedback you receive will insure identification of the skills involved in arranging an appointment. We suggest that you practice until you have role-played the skill perfectly for two situations in a row. Below is an example of what might occur during a role-playing situation.

ROLE-PLAYING NARRATIVE   REFERRAL BEHAVIOR

Partner: Here's the description of a practice situation: Assume that a teen-ager has come to you with a story about how his father, who has a drinking problem, beats the boy's mother and younger brother. You have found that the social service directory lists ALA-NON as an agency that provides support for the families of alcoholics. I'll play the part of the staff at ALA-NON.

Helper: I dial the phone number for ALA-NON and the phone rings.   Call the agency

Partner: Good morning, ALA-NON. May I help you?

Helper: Hello, my name is *(student's name)*.   State name and affiliation
I am working for *(student's affiliation)*. I have a client whose father has a drinking   State client's problem
problem. When he is drunk, he beats the boy's mother and younger brother. Could   Request help
you help with this problem?

Partner: That sounds like the type of problem that we specialize in. We would be glad to try to help the family.

Helper: Could I schedule an appointment   Request an appointment
time for my client to come in to talk to you about the problem?

Partner: Okay, my schedule is open all afternoon.

Helper: Could he see you at 2:30?

Partner: Yes, that would be fine.

Helper: (to client) Can you go to ALA-NON   Ask client if time
at 2:30 this afternoon?   is convenient

Partner: Sure, I can do that.

Helper: 2:30 this afternoon would be fine with my client. Who should I have him ask for?

Partner: My name is *(partner's name)*.

Helper: Great, he'll be there this afternoon.   Thank the person
Thanks for your help.

In this situation, the partner should check off all of the referral behaviors involved in arranging an appointment as being performed correctly. The partner should also let the student know that all of the steps were done correctly. We recommend that the role-playing partner should feel free to compliment the student for things done well and explain ways that performance might be improved.

Below are several role-playing situations. The partner should read the situational description to you and you should practice arranging an appointment for the client. You and your partner should each feel free to make up any necessary information.

Assume that a teen-ager has come to you with a story about how his father, who has a drinking problem, beats the boy's mother and younger brother. You have found that the social service directory lists ALA-NON as an agency that provides support for the families of alcoholics.

Assume that a young woman with three small children has come to you for help in paying her rent. The social service directory lists The Women's Center as one agency that offers help for this problem.

Assume that a man has come to you with a consumer product complaint. He purchased a used refrigerator that does not work. You have found that the Office of Consumer Affairs handles this type of problem.

Assume that a woman with a three-year-old daughter has come to you for help. Her daughter has not yet started to talk and she is worried that the girl might have a hearing problem. You have found that the Department of Health offers free speech and hearing services for children.

Assume that a man has come in and explained that he was laid off work and needs enough groceries for his family to eat until he receives his first unemployment compensation check. You have found that the Emergency Services Council can help by providing enough food for the family to eat for one week.

Assume that your client is an elderly man who has been placed on a special diet that he cannot prepare for himself. You have found that Meals on Wheels has a service that might solve his problem.

CHECKLIST:
ARRANGING AN APPOINTMENT FOR A CLIENT

1. Call the agency.

2. State name and affiliation.

3. State the client's problem.

4. Request help from the agency.

5. Request an appointment.

6. Ask the client if the appointment time is convenient.

7. Thank the person.

Chapter 7

COMPLETING AN
INTERAGENCY REFERRAL FORM

Obtaining feedback on the success of your referrals is one of the most important aspects of an information and referral service. If your clients do not receive the help needed to solve their problems, you have not done them a service by providing the referral. You have merely taken up more of their time sending them to another agency that is unable to help. This chapter describes how to complete an interagency referral form. Use of an interagency referral form will allow you to determine whether your clients received the help they need.

The referral form described in this chapter was developed for use by social service agencies in Lawrence, Kansas. If your agency has decided to adapt the form for use in your community, it is important that you take note of the changes in the form. However, the general procedure for form completion described here should be helpful in completing any interagency referral form.

An interagency referral form can serve four functions: (1) it provides a record of the referrals provided by the agency; (2) it serves as a reminder of the appointment for the client; (3) it provides information to the helping agency about the services needed by the client; and (4) it serves as a prompt to obtain follow-up information about the services received by the client. Therefore, by completing the interagency referral form, you provide assistance to your agency, the client, and the agency to which you refer the client.

We recommend that you complete an interagency referral form whenever you send a client to another agency to receive a service not provided by your agency. This includes referrals provided for walk-in and telephone clients. The following are examples of when to complete an interagency referral form:

(1) Mrs. Williams needs weather stripping on her home and your agency does not provide this service.
(2) Bob Sims needs a small cash loan which is not available through your agency.
(3) Wilma Helms needs a winter coat and your agency does not operate a clothing program.

We recommend that you perform the following nine activities when completing an interagency referral form: complete the client information; complete the referral agency information; complete the helping agency information; complete the appointment information; complete the reason for referral; give the client a copy of the referral form; thank the client and request future contact; send the helping agency copy and the feedback copy to the helping agency; and file the original copy of the referral form. Each of these steps is described in detail in this chapter.

COMPLETE THE CLIENT INFORMATION

We recommend that you fill in the client's name, address, and phone number on the blank lines provided in the upper left-hand corner of the referral form. In some cases, a client may be unwilling to give you this information. If a client considers the problem to be so confidential that she/he is unwilling to tell you a name, address, or phone number, then leave this space blank and complete the remainder of the form. Two examples of how this information might look are provided below:

Client's name	*Bill Smith*	Client's name	*Mary Allen*
Address	*1312 Iowa*	Address	*437 Tyler*
Phone	*842-8288*	Phone	*No phone*

Completing the client information will provide a record of who is being referred to the helping agency.

COMPLETE THE REFERRAL AGENCY INFORMATION

We suggest that you complete the information about the referral agency with the name, address, and telephone number of the agency where you work. Next, you should write your name on the line labelled "Referred By" and the day's date on the line provided. The space for this information is found in the left center portion of the referral form. Sample referral agency listings are provided below:

Referral Agency	*South Side Center*	Referral Agency	*Self Help Inc.*
Address	*3712 S. 7th*	Address	*935 Mass.*
Phone	*993-5491*	Phone	*237-9421*
Referred By	*Velma Gold*	Referred By	*Bill Robinson*
Date	*4/14/81*	Date	*Dec. 16, 1982*

This information will be helpful for the agency to which the client is referred. It will make it possible for the helping agency to call if additional information about the client or the problem is required.

COMPLETE THE HELPING AGENCY INFORMATION

After you have determined which agency can help the client, and you have confirmed the information with the helping agency, we suggest that you complete the information about the helping agency. This involves filling in the name, address, and phone number of the agency to which you are sending the client on the blank lines provided in the right center portion of the interagency referral form. For example, two ways you might fill in the information are as follows:

Agency Referred to	*Valley View Cent.*	Agency Referred to	*Iowa House*
Address	*312 Valley View Rd.*	Address	*1212 Iowa*
Phone	*888-9391*	Phone	*691-2990*

This information will help the client locate the agency and allow your agency to obtain follow-up information on service delivery.

COMPLETE THE APPOINTMENT WITH INFORMATION

The preceding chapter (Chapter 6) described a procedure for scheduling an appointment for a client with the helping agency. Information obtained in such telephone conversations should be

included in this section. We recommend that you fill in the name of
the person with whom the appointment is made, the day of the week
for which the appointment is made, the date of the appointment, and
the time of the appointment (including a.m. or p.m.) on the blanks
provided directly below the "Agency Referred To" information. For
examples:

Appointment with	*Selma Snow*			Appointment with	*Julie Howell*	
Day of Week	*Monday*			Day of Week	*Thursday*	
Date	*8/19/81*			Date	*10/7/80*	
Time	*9:00* [x]	[ ]		Time	*2:30* [ ]	[x]
	a.m	p.m.			a.m.	p.m.

This information lets the client know when to go for the appointment
and who to ask for upon arrival. In addition, in this way you will be
able to check back with the specific person who was to help the client
to receive information on service delivery.

COMPLETE THE REASON FOR REFERRAL

We suggest that you describe the service needed by the client in the
space marked "Reason for Referral." In addition, we have found that
it is often useful to provide a brief description of the circumstances
that caused the problem. It is important to take care and not write
below the last line of the reason for referral. This space will be used
for feedback from the helping agency. An example of a reason for
referral is provided below:

> Reason for Referral *Emergency Food—person laid off work and has
> two small children. Has applied for unemployment, but it will be at
> least one more week before food money is available.*

This information will let the helping agency know why the client was
referred.

GIVE THE CLIENT A COPY OF THE
INTERAGENCY REFERRAL FORM

We recommend that you give the client a copy of the referral form.
This is possible if your agency is using a multiple-copy type of
interagency referral form. If not, we suggest that you make a note of
the appointment information for the client. Giving the client a copy

of the referral information increases the chances that the client will know where to go, when to go there, and who to see once she/he has arrived.

THANK THE CLIENT AND REQUEST FUTURE CONTACT

We have found that it is important to thank the client by name for coming to the agency for help. It is also helpful to state that you would like them to come back again. Several examples of how you might thank a client and request future contact are provided below:

(1) "Thank you, Mrs. Smith. I hope that you come back whenever you need help with another problem."
(2) "Bill, I'm glad you came in. Come back again any time."

This kind of positive statement lets the client know that you are glad to help and are willing to serve the person again in the future. This can be especially important when you have provided a referral, rather than helping the person by providing a direct service. If, for some reason, the problem was not solved, the client may be more likely to return to you for additional help.

SEND THE HELPING AGENCY COPY AND THE FEEDBACK COPY TO THE HELPING AGENCY

We have found that it is useful to remove the helping agency copy and the feedback copy of the interagency referral form. These copies can be placed in an envelope addressed to the helping agency and sent out with the next day's mail. If you commonly provide several referrals to the same agency, you might decide to hold the referral forms to be sent out together. Mailing the helping agency copy provides the agency with information about the client that has been referred to them for help. The feedback copy can be completed and returned to provide your agency with information about the services received by the client.

FILE THE ORIGINAL COPY

We recommend that you file your agency's copy of the interagency referral form. If the form is filed in a calendar file, the information can be easily retrieved for follow-up. Some agencies will file the referral form until one week after the date of the client's appointment.

If the feedback portion of the form had not been returned, they would call the helping agency to find out if the client had arrived and received the necessary services. This copy of the referral form provides information about who was referred, what agency they were referred to, and what type of service they needed.

In summary, we recommend the following steps in completing an interagency referral form:

(1) complete the client information
(2) complete the referral agency information
(3) complete the helping agency information
(4) complete the appointment information
(5) complete the reason for referral
(6) give the client a copy of the interagency referral form
(7) thank the client and request future contact
(8) send the helping agency copy and the feedback copy to the helping agency
(9) file the original copy.

STUDY GUIDE:
COMPLETING AN INTERAGENCY REFERRAL FORM

1. Describe four functions of an interagency referral form.

2. When should you complete an interagency referral form?

3. Describe the activities involved in completing an interagency referral form.

4. How can an interagency referral form be used to obtain client follow-up information?

STUDY GUIDE ANSWER KEY:
COMPLETING AN INTERAGENCY REFERRAL FORM

1. Four functions of an interagency referral form include:
    (a) record of referrals provided by your agency
    (b) an appointment reminder for the client
    (c) information about the client's problem for use by the helping agency
    (d) a prompt to obtain follow-up information.
2. An interagency referral form should be completed whenever a client is referred to another agency.
3. The activities involved in completing an interagency referral form include:
    (a) complete client information
    (b) complete the referral agency information
    (c) complete the helping agency information
    (d) complete the appointment information
    (e) complete the reason for referral
    (f) give the client a copy of the interagency referral form
    (g) thank the client and request future contact
    (h) send the helping agency copy and the feedback copy to the helping agency
    (i) file the original copy.
4. Filing the original copy of the interagency referral form in a calendar file will enable you to retrieve the referral information one week after the client's appointment to check with the helping agency on the services rendered to the client.

SITUATIONAL EXAMPLE:
COMPLETING AN INTERAGENCY REFERRAL FORM

Complete the interagency referral form as you might if you were providing a referral for the client described below. Check your answers after you have completed the form.

Situation: Mary McCarthy, age 97, came in to the Help-U Center and wanted some information on where she could get storm windows placed on her house for the winter. Mary's address is 819 W. 7th Street. Her phone number is 851-0291. The address of the Help-U Center is 2002 Elm Street and their phone is 852-8754. Assume that you are filling out the referral form and are referring her to the County Council on Aging. Their address is 917½ Union Street and the phone number is 842-6336. Mary has an appointment with Sam Stone on Monday, November 16, at 10:00 a.m.

INTERAGENCY REFERRAL
FORM

Client's Name_____
Address_____
Phone_____

Referral Agency_____   Agency Referred to_____
Address_____   Address_____
Phone_____   Phone_____
Referred by_____   Appointment with_____
Date_____   Day of Week_____
                                         Date_____
                                         Time_____[ ] [ ]
                                                     a.m. p.m.

REASON FOR REFERRAL:_____
_____
_____

Describe what you should do:
1. Thank the client and request future contact:_____
_____
_____

SITUATIONAL EXAMPLE ANSWER KEY
COMPLETING AN INTERAGENCY REFERRAL FORM

INTERAGENCY
REFERRAL FORM

Client's Name *Mary McCarthy*
Address *819 W. 7th*
Phone *851-0291*

Referral Agency *Help-U Center*   Agency Referred *County Council*
Address *2002 Elm*   to *on Aging*
Phone *852-8754*   Address *917½ Union*
Referred by *(your name)*   Phone *842-6336*
Date *(today's date)*   Appointment with *Sam Stone*
                                     Day of Week *Monday*
                                     Date *November 16*
                                     Time *10:00* [x] [ ]
                                                   a.m. p.m.

REASON FOR REFERRAL: *Storm windows placed on her house for the winter.*

1. *Thank the client and request future contact.*
   Sample Answer: "Thank you for coming in today, Mary. Stop back and see us again."

SITUATIONS TO PRACTICE COMPLETING AN
INTERAGENCY REFERRAL FORM

This section is provided to give you an opportunity to practice completing interagency referral forms. Below are several referral situations that might occur. For each situation, assume that your agency does not offer the needed service. Complete an interagency referral form (provided on the following pages) for each client situation. Information about the helping agency can be obtained from the community service directory developed for your community. Similarly, use your own name and the information about the agency at which you work to describe the referral agency.

Ron Williams has come to you for help with a family problem. His father, who has a drinking problem, beats Ron's mother and younger brother. Ron, whose telephone number is 754-0098, lives at 6794 West Hillside.

Betty Freed lives at 830 Ohio. She has no telephone. She has come to you for help in paying this month's rent.

Charles Underwood has come to you for help with a consumer problem. He paid for a used refrigerator and was told that it would work. However, when the seller delivered it to his home (98 East Orange), he found that its freezer did not function. Charles's telephone number is 961-6443.

Becky Brown has a three-year-old daughter named Betty. Betty has not yet learned to talk. The Browns live at 302 Kam Avenue. Their telephone number is 524-4550.

Cal Fuller, of 839 Sheridan, was laid off from his job at Goodyear Tire Company. He needs enough food to get his family through the weekend, until he receives his first unemployment check. Cal's telephone number is 262-8678.

INTERAGENCY REFERRAL
        FORM

Client's Name
      Address
      Phone

Referral Agency_____   Agency Referred to_____
        Address_____   Address_____
          Phone_____   Phone_____
      Referred by_____   Appointment with_____
          Date_____   Day of Week_____
                                              Date_____
                                              Time_____[ ] [ ]
                                                          a.m. p.m.

REASON FOR REFERRAL:_____
_____
_____

INTERAGENCY REFERRAL
        FORM

Client's Name
      Address
      Phone

Referral Agency_____   Agency Referred to_____
        Address_____   Address_____
          Phone_____   Phone_____
      Referred by_____   Appointment with_____
          Date_____   Day of Week_____
                                              Date_____
                                              Time_____[ ] [ ]
                                                          a.m. p.m.

REASON FOR REFERRAL:_____
_____
_____

INTERAGENCY REFERRAL FORM

Client's Name _____
    Address _____
    Phone _____

Referral Agency _____   Agency Referred to _____
    Address _____   Address _____
    Phone _____   Phone _____
    Referred by _____   Appointment with _____
    Date _____   Day of Week _____
     Date _____
     Time _____ [ ] [ ]
     a.m.   p.m.

REASON FOR REFERRAL: _____
_____
_____

INTERAGENCY REFERRAL FORM

Client's Name
    Address
    Phone

Referral Agency _____   Agency Referred to _____
    Address _____   Address _____
    Phone _____   Phone _____
    Referred by _____   Appointment with _____
    Date _____   Day of Week _____
     Date _____
     Time _____ [ ] [ ]
     a.m.   p.m.

REASON FOR REFERRAL: _____
_____
_____

INTERAGENCY REFERRAL
     FORM

Client's Name _____
     Address _____
     Phone _____

Referral Agency   Agency Referred to
     Address   Address
     Phone   Phone
  Referred by   Appointment with
     Date   Day of Week
                                   Date
                                   Time_____[ ] [ ]
                                           a.m. p.m.

REASON FOR REFERRAL:_____
_____
_____

INTERAGENCY REFERRAL
     FORM

Client's Name
     Address
     Phone

Referral Agency   Agency Referred to
     Address   Address
     Phone   Phone
  Referred by   Appointment with
     Date   Day of Week
                                   Date
                                   Time_____[ ] [ ]
                                           a.m. p.m.

REASON FOR REFERRAL:_____
_____
_____

CHECKLIST:
COMPLETING AN INTERAGENCY REFERRAL FORM

1. Complete the client information.

2. Complete the referral agency information.

3. Complete the helping agency information.

4. Complete the appointment information.

5. Complete the reason for referral.

6. Give the client a copy of the interagency referral form.

7. Thank the client and request future contact.

8. Send the helping agency copy and the feedback copy to the helping agency.

9. File the original copy.

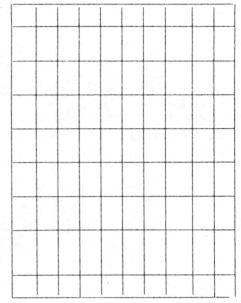

Chapter 8

HANDLING SPECIAL PROBLEMS IN
PROVIDING A REFERRAL

There are occasions in which a person will have a problem that does not seem to be listed in the social service directory. This may occur because either no service agency currently handles the problem or the service was overlooked when the social service directory was developed. Difficulty in locating an agency that offers a service does not make the problem go away. Take heart, this chapter is designed to provide a few hints on helping clients when there is a special problem in providing a referral.

In trying to provide a referral, you may come to a dead-end when searching through the social service directory for an appropriate service. Perhaps the index contains no headings for the client's problem; maybe the problem-service cards show no available help for the client; or perhaps the client does not seem to be eligible for the services of any local agency. What do you do if the directory does not list any agency that can help a client pay her income tax, find a job, or locate a place to spend the night? What should you do if someone comes to you in need of volunteer workers to clean the neighborhood and you cannot find any appropriate listing?

We have found the following activities to be helpful in solving problems that do not seem to be listed in the directory: check any appropriate problem headings; check any appropriate group headings; ask other staff members; and ask the staff of another agency. Each of these problem-solving methods is described in greater detail in this chapter.

CHECK ANY APPROPRIATE PROBLEM HEADINGS

We have found that it is often helpful to check the index for listings that are similar to the client's problem. It is important to check under every feasible index listing to help the client solve the problem. Take the example of a man who came to you for help in paying his water bill. If you looked in the index under WATER and MONEY, but found no help for the client, do not give up. You might then check under related headings such as Economic Assistance, Financial Assistance, or Utilities. Checking every possible heading that is related to the problem will increase the likelihood finding help for your client.

If you are successful in locating a referral source with any step listed in this chapter, omit the other activities included in the chapter and follow the regular referral procedures. However, if one activity was not effective in solving the client's problem, then proceed to the next recommendation.

CHECK ANY APPROPRIATE GROUP HEADINGS

For some problems it is possible to find help by looking in the index for general, non-problem-specific categories that might describe the *client* rather than the service. Some agencies describe their services by the age, sex, or background of their clientele. The index of the social service directory might have a listing that describes the client. Examples of general group headings include: Alcoholics, Elderly, Mentally Retarded, Students, Veterans, and Women. Checking for any appropriate group headings might result in finding an agency that has a particular interest in serving your client.

ASK OTHER STAFF MEMBERS

Another option is to ask other staff members at your agency if they have any ideas as to who might be able to help the client. We have found that if the directory is not helpful, sometimes other people at the agency might be. For example, you might ask a coworker:

Do you know of any agency that can help with getting a dead tree removed from Mr. Smith's yard? If something isn't done, it's going to fall on his house. However, I haven't been able to locate any help in the social service directory.

There will be times when other staff members at your agency will have information that is not currently listed in the directory. This can occur when the problem is one that is not common and no one thought of describing the service when the social service directory was developed.

ASK THE STAFF FROM ANOTHER AGENCY

When nothing else has helped, we suggest that you call on the staff of another agency for help in locating assistance. Even if the agency you call for help does not handle the problem, they might be able to help you locate an agency that can solve the problem. It is often best to call an agency that deals with problems similar to that experienced by the client or an agency that specializes in working with clients that are like your client. If you have an elderly client who is in need of help not offered by any agency listed in the directory and no one from your agency has any suggestions for help, you might call on the staff from a local agency that specializes in services for the aging. Similarly, you might call on a local garden shop for a client needing a part-time gardener. Often someone who handles similar problems will be able to provide information about hard to find services.

If you are unable to help the client find a needed service in any of these ways, we suggest that you explain to the client that you have found no help, but that you will continue to look—*then continue to look.* Once you are able to find someone who can help, contact the client with the new information.

In summary, the four steps that we recommend when you have difficulty in providing a referral include:

(1) check any appropriate problem heading
(2) check any appropriate group heading
(3) ask other staff members
(4) ask the staff of another agency.

STUDY GUIDE:
HANDLING SPECIAL PROBLEMS IN
PROVIDING A REFERRAL

1. Describe three circumstances which would present a problem in providing a referral.

2. Describe what might be done to handle a referral if no agency appears to offer the needed assistance.

STUDY GUIDE ANSWER KEY:
HANDLING SPECIAL PROBLEMS IN
PROVIDING A REFERRAL

1. Circumstances that might present a special problem in providing a
    referral include:
    (a) no service agency currently handles the problem
    (b) the service was overlooked when the social service directory
         was developed
    (c) the index contains no headings for the client's problem
    (d) the problem-service cards show no available help for the client
    (e) the client does not seem to be eligible for the services of any
         agency.
2. Activities that might be performed to handle a referral if no agency
    appears to offer the needed assistance include:
    (a) check any appropriate problem headings
    (b) check any appropriate group headings
    (c) ask other staff members
    (d) ask the staff from another agency.

SITUATIONAL EXAMPLE:
HANDLING SPECIAL PROBLEMS IN
PROVIDING A REFERRAL

Situation: You are working in the Office of Social Services. A
young woman with two children comes in to tell you that she has just
gotten a night job. She needs to find a regular babysitter for her two-
year-old twins. The first place you looked in the social service
directory index was Babysitting, but the index referred you to Child
Care. Under Child Care (Part Day) and Child Care (Full Day), five
agencies were listed. The first listing was the Douglas County Health
Department. You turned to the agency card for the Health Department, looked up their telephone number, and called Kay Kent at
843-0721. After identifying yourself and explaining the problem,
Kay told you that they had no listings for all-night babysitters. You
then followed this procedure for each of the other four agencies listed
under Child Care, but had no luck finding all-night babysitters.

Please fill in each blank with an appropriate answer. Use the answer key to check your answers.

1. Check any appropriate problem headings (An index is provided below)

Index

Adoption	Child Care (Part Day)	Hearing Problems
Babysitting (see Child	Child Care (Full Day)	Legal Problems
Care)	Clothing	Police Problems
Birth Control	Elderly	Utilities

Write any appropriate problem headings here:_____

_____

2. Check any appropriate group headings.
Write any appropriate group headings here:_____

_____

3. Ask other staff members.
You might ask Jill, another staff member:_____

_____

Jill told you that she had no ideas, that nobody she knew would want to sit for two-year-old twins all night.

4. Ask the staff of another agency.
In this instance you might call another multiservice agency that handles lots of different problems. Write what you might say when you call.

_____

_____

_____

_____

SITUATIONAL EXAMPLE ANSWER KEY:
HANDLING SPECIAL PROBLEMS IN
PROVIDING A REFERRAL

1. *Check any appropriate problem headings.*

There are no appropriate problem headings other than Child Care and Babysitting (which you have already checked).

2. *Check any appropriate group headings.*

There are no appropriate group headings listed in this index.

3. *Ask other staff members.*

Sample Answer: "Jill, do you know of any overnight childcare facilities? I have already checked with all the agencies listed in the card file."

4. *Ask the staff of another agency.*

Sample answer: "This is *(your name)* from the Office of Social Services. We have a woman who has just gotten a night job and she needs someone to care for her two-year-old twins during her work hours. We have already checked at_____,
_____, and_____,
but no one seems to be able to help. Do you have any ideas as to who might be able to help?"

Chapter 9

PUTTING IT ALL TOGETHER

The preceding chapters have described a process that we have found useful in providing information and referral services. These chapters have described how to use the social service directory, schedule an appointment for a client, complete an interagency referral form, and handle special problems. Though the skills were dealt with separately in the earlier chapters, this chapter should illustrate how all of the skills might fit together in an everyday referral situation.

Once you have determined that a client's problem cannot be handled by your agency, we recommend that you:

1. Complete the client information portion of the interagency referral form.

This involves filling in the client's name, address, and phone number on the referral form.

2. Complete the referral agency information portion of the interagency referral form.

This involves filling in the name and phone number of the referral agency (where you work), writing your name on the line labelled "Referred by," and noting the day's date on the referral form.

3. Complete the reason for referral on the interagency referral form.

This involves writing the reason that you are referring the client to the second agency. This section should describe a service that is needed by the client.

4. Ask the client to wait while you use the directory to locate an agency that can help.

This involves requesting that the client wait while you look up the information on the client's problem.

5. Match the client's problem to a social service directory index listing.

This involves looking through the index for the client's problem.

6. Write all possible problem-service listings on scratch paper.

This involves writing each potentially appropriate problem or service category (from the index) on scratch paper. If the index does not list any appropriate services, you should check for other categories or services, or headings that might describe the client. If this fails, do not be afraid to check with the staff at your agency or other helping agencies to find someone who can offer the needed service.

7. Turn to the problem-service card.

This involves turning to the first problem-service file card listed on the sheet of scratch paper. The problem-service cards are provided in alphabetical order in the social service directory.

8. Determine if the service offered is what the client needs.

This involves reading the description of the problem handled and deciding if that is the client's problem. If the service does not meet the client's needs, check another problem-service listing.

9. If the service offered matches the client's need, then write the agency name on scratch paper.

This involves writing on scratch paper the name of any potentially appropriate agencies listed at the bottom of the problem-service card.

10. Turn to the agency card and determine the client's eligibility.

This involves looking at the eligibility requirements on the agency card to see if the client meets all of the requirements.

11. If the client is eligible for the service, then call the agency.

This involves dialing the telephone number of the agency. This number is listed on the agency card located in the referral file.

12. State your name and affiliation.

This involves telling the person your name and the name of the agency where you work.

13. State client's problem.

This involves explaining that you have a client who needs assistance and stating exactly what is needed.

14. Request help from the agency.

This involves asking if the agency can assist in solving the client's problem.

If the agency cannot provide the service, close the conversation and return to the social service directory to find an agency that can help.

15. If the agency can provide the service, request an appointment for the client.

This involves asking the person at the agency to schedule an appointment for the client. The appointment should be at a specific time, on a specific day, and with a specific person.

16. Ask the client if the appointment time is convenient.

This involves asking the client if he or she will be able to go to the agency at the appointment time.

17. Confirm the appointment.

This involves telling the person at the referral agency whether the appointment time is acceptable to the client. It is important to work with the client and the helping agency until you have scheduled an appointment time that is convenient for both.

18. Complete the appointment information on the interagency referral form.

This involves filling in the name of the person with whom the appointment is made as well as the day of the week, date, and time (including a.m. or p.m.) of the appointment on the interagency referral form.

19. Complete the helping agency information.

This involves filling in the name of the agency that is to help the client, as well as the agency's address and phone number on the interagency referral form.

20. Thank the person.

This involves expressing your appreciation to the person at the helping agency for his or her assistance.

21. Give the client a copy of the interagency referral form.

This involves removing the completed client's copy and giving it to the client.

22. Thank the client and request future contact.

This involves thanking the client by name and stating that you would like him or her to come back again.

23. Send the helping agency copy and the feedback copy to the helping agency.

This involves placing the two copies of the referral form in an envelope addressed to the receiving agency and mailing it. This can be done on an individual basis or you can save up referrals for one agency and mail out all of the referrals to that agency at the end of the day or week.

24. File the original copy of the interagency referral form.

This involves placing the completed referral form in the file for referrals.

We have included an opportunity to practice all of the activities required to provide a referral. We have structured a review criterion test for this purpose. This review contains a small social service directory and an example of a client problem.

REVIEW CRITERION TEST

CRITERION TEST INSTRUCTIONS

This section is designed to provide an evaluation of your performance of all of the skills associated with providing information and referral. You should answer all of the questions without looking at the answer key. Grade your answers after you have completed the entire test. Reread the appropriate sections of the book to obtain information to correct any incorrect answers. If you answer seven or more questions incorrectly, reread all of Part II and retake the Review Criterion Test. Following these instructions will help insure that you have acquired all of the skills needed to provide information and referral.

Since the review criterion test is in a written format, it is impossible to demonstrate exactly how you would act in an actual referral situation. However, this test does attempt to approximate that situation. Please fill in the blank beside each referral activity with an *example* of what you would say or do. For example, you might respond to the item, "Ask the client to wait" with the example answer, "Would you please wait for a moment?". This answer would be scored as correct. The activity, Complete the client information, might be followed by the example answer, "Bill Jones, 1034 Pennsylvania, 842-6919." This would be scored as correct only if it was the client's name, address, and phone number. In summary, write out an example of the referral activities required for each item on the criterion test.

Below is all of the information needed to provide a referral. We have provided client information, index listings, problem-service cards, and agency cards. Use these materials to answer the review criterion test questions.

SITUATION DESCRIPTION FOR CRITERION TEST

Linda Johnson, who lives just down the street at 2121 East Lawn, has come to Help-U Center to ask for assistance with a problem. Her doctor has prescribed an antibiotic for her sick child, but Linda is unable to pay for the medicine. She has brought the prescription with her. Linda's phone number is 842-9186.

INDEX FOR REVIEW CRITERION TEST

ADULT EDUCATION

BIRTH CONTROL
information
medical

CHILD CARE
babysitter referrals
full-day child care
part-day child care

COUNSELING
budget
child abuse
welfare

ELDERLY
housing
medical
yardwork

HEARING
children
problems

HOUSING ASSISTANCE
permanent
temporary

MEDICAL
children
home health
prescriptions
transportation

POLICE PROBLEMS

TRANSPORTATION
in town
out of town

PROBLEM-SERVICE CARDS FOR
REVIEW CRITERION TEST

BIRTH CONTROL (Medical)

Problem Handled: Counseling, physical examinations, and prescriptions for full range of contraceptives.

Contact: County Health Dept.

COUNSELING (Child Abuse)

Problem Handled: Provide psychological evaluation and therapy for child abusers.

Contact: Mental Health Association Volunteers, Inc.

COUNSELING (Welfare)

Problem Handled: Help in budgeting money on a fixed income.

Contact: Help-U Center Mental Health Association New York House

---

ELDERLY (Medical)

Problem Handled: Residents of county may receive blood pressure check, flu shots, and bandage changes.

Contact: County Health Department

HEARING (Children)

Problem Handled: Provide hearing test and information about hearing aids.

Contact: Speech and Hearing Clinic

MEDICAL (Children)

Problem Handled: Well child clinic provides immunizations and physical examinations.

Contact: County Health Department

MEDICAL (Prescriptions)

Problem Handled: Need a prescription filled in an emergency. Not for ongoing problems where prescription needs to be refilled again and again.

Contact: New York House

TRANSPORTATION
(In Town)

Problem Handled: In-town transportation provided by volunteers.

Contact: Help-U Center

AGENCY CARDS FOR REVIEW CRITERION TEST

COUNTY HEALTH DEPARTMENT

Address: 3121 West 9th
Phone: 841-1111
Hours: 8:00-5:00 M-F

Eligibility: County Residents

Appointments: Yes

HELP-U CENTER

Address: 2110 East Lawn
Phone: 843-3131
Hours: 8:00-6:00 M-F

Eligibility: Anyone

Appointments: Yes

MENTAL HEALTH ASSOCIATION

Address: 923 Western
Phone: 842-1164
Hours: 9:00-5:00 M-S

Eligibility: Must be over 18

Appointments: Yes

NEW YORK HOUSE

Address: 1221 New York
Phone: 842-0440
Hours: 8-5, M-F

Eligibility: Anyone

Appointments: Yes

SPEECH AND HEARING CLINIC

Address: 1210 Hilltop
Phone: 864-3404
Hours: 1-3 p.m. Weds.

Eligibility: Must be under 12

Appointments: Yes

VOLUNTEERS, INC.

Address: 101 Maine
Phone: 843-3210
Hours: 9:00-4:00, M-F

Eligibility: Anyone

Appointments: Yes

REVIEW CRITERION TEST

1. Complete the client information.
   Client's Name_____
        Address_____
          Phone_____

2. Complete the referral agency information.
   Referral Agency_____
          Address_____
            Phone_____

3. Complete the reason for referral.
   Reason for referral:_____
   _____
   _____

4. Ask the client to wait.
   _____
   _____
   _____

5. Match the client's problem to an index listing.
   _____
   _____
   _____

6. Write all possible problem-service listings.
   _____
   _____
   _____

7. Turn to the problem-service card.
   _____
   _____
   _____

8. Determine if the service offered is what the client needs.
   _____
   _____
   _____

9. If the service offered matches the client's need, write the agency name._____
_____
_____

10. Turn to the agency card and determine client's eligibility.
_____
_____
_____

11. If the client is eligible for the service, then call the agency.
_____
_____
_____

The person answers the phone and says, "Hello, this is Gail Windy."
12. State name and affiliation.
_____
_____
_____

13. State client's problem.
_____
_____

14. Request help from agency.
_____
_____
_____

Gail says, "Sure, we would be glad to help out."
15. Request an appointment time.
_____
_____
_____

Gail says, "I can schedule the appointment for Thursday, October 23, at 2:30 with Bill Byers."

16. Ask client if appointment time is convenient.

_____

_____

The client says, "That time is fine with me."

17. Confirm the appointment.

_____

18. Complete the appointment with information.
    Appointment with_____
        Day of Week_____
            Date_____
            Time_____ [ ]   [ ]
                                        a.m.   p.m.

19. Complete the helping agency information.
    Agency Referred to_____
            Address_____
            Phone_____

20. Thank the person.

_____

_____

21. Give the client a copy of the interagency referral form.

_____

_____

22. Thank the client and request future contact.

_____

_____

_____

23. Send the helping agency copy and the feedback copy to the helping agency.

24. File the original copy of the interagency referral form.

ANSWER KEY: REVIEW CRITERION TEST

The answer key provides an appropriate example for each question. Your answer does not have to be in the same words, merely the same in meaning.

1. Complete the client information.
   Client's name *Linda Johnson*
         Address *2121 East Lawn*
         Phone *842-9186*

2. Complete the referral agency information.
   Referral Agency *Help U Center*
         Address *2110 East Lawn*
         Phone *842-9186*

3. Complete the reason for referral.
   Reason for referral: *Needs a prescription for antibiotics filled for her sick child.*

4. Ask the client to wait.
   Sample Answer: "Would you please wait one moment while I try to find an agency that will be able to help?"

5. Match the client's problem to an index listing.
   Sample Answer: "I would look at each listing to find one that is for filling a prescription."

6. Write all possible problem-service listings.
   Sample Answer: "I would list MEDICAL-prescription." NOTE: If you have written other listings, that is all right, but you should have Medical-prescription written down.

7. Turn to the problem-service card.
   Sample Answer: "I would turn to the card for Medical-prescription."

8. Determine if the service offered is what the client needs.
   Sample Answer: "This is a service needed by the client."

9. If the service offered matches the client's need, write the agency name.
   Sample Answer: "New York House"

10. Turn to the agency card and determine client's eligibility.
Sample Answer: "The client is eligible."

11. If the client is eligible for the service, then call the agency.
Sample Answer: "I would call New York House at 842-0440."

12. State name and affiliation.
Sample Answer: "Hello, this is *(your name)* from Help-U Center."

13. State client's problem.
Sample Answer: "I have a client who needs to have an antibiotic prescription filled for her child. My client cannot afford to pay to have it filled."

14. Request help from agency.
Sample Answer: "Will you be able to help with this problem?"

15. Request an appointment time.
Sample Answer: "When could Linda come in for an appointment?"

16. Ask client if appointment time is convenient.
Sample Answer: "Linda, is 2:30 Thursday, October 23 all right?"

17. Confirm the appointment.
Sample Answer: "She said that would be fine."

18. Complete the appointment with information.
Appointment with *Bill Byers*
    Day of Week *Thursday*
        Date *October 23*
        Time *2:30*   [ ] [x]
                          a.m. p.m.

19. Complete the helping agency information.
Agency Referred to *New York House*
        Address *1221 New York*
        Phone *842-0440*

20. Thank the person.
  Sample Answer: "Thanks a lot for your help, Gail."

21. Give the client a copy of the interagency referral form.
  Sample Answer: "Here is a copy of the referral form for you. It tells you where you should go and who to see."

22. Thank the client and request future contact.
  Sample Answer: "Thanks for coming in, Linda. Please feel free to come back any time."

23. Send the helping agency copy and the feedback copy to the helping agency.
  Sample Answer: "I would place the yellow and gold copies of the referral form in an envelope to send to New York House."

24. File the original copy of the interagency referral form.
  Sample Answer: "I would place the original copy in the referral file."

SITUATIONS TO PRACTICE PROVIDING A REFERRAL

Now that you have completed each of the lessons for how to provide a referral, we suggest that you and your partner practice putting all of the referral behaviors together. We have included several novel referral situations in which you can practice providing referrals. In these situations your partner will need to play the part of the client and the part of the person you contact at the helping agency.

In each situation we suggest that you assume that you work for an organization that does not offer the service needed by the client. Use the social service directory that has been developed for your community to locate the appropriate helping agency, complete an interagency referral form for the referral situation, and practice arranging an appointment for the client. Feel free to make up additional referral situations if you wish to continue practicing the referral skills. It would be helpful if your partner would vary his or her responses to your inquiries so that you can gain practice dealing with a variety of referral situations.

A man has come to you for help in finding a job. He is willing to do any kind of work. However, he needs to earn enough to support his two children.

A 15-year-old unwed girl is pregnant and has come to you for help. She lives at home and has not told her parents about the pregnancy. She has no idea what she should do about her situation.

A retired factory worker, who is living on a small pension, requires an operation. However, he has no medical benefits and cannot afford to pay for the surgery.

A young woman, living on her own for the first time, has come for help in budgeting her money. She likes her present job and believes that they pay her a reasonable salary. However, she always seems to be broke.

An elderly woman, who lives alone in her own house, has come to you for help. Her front porch has caved in and she has no way of repairing it.

A person needs a ride to the doctor's office for an appointment.

INTERAGENCY REFERRAL
        FORM

Client's Name
    Address
    Phone

Referral Agency   Agency Referred to
    Address   Address
    Phone   Phone
    Referred by   Appointment with
    Date   Day of Week
                                                    Date
                                                    Time_____[ ] [ ]
                                                                a.m.   p.m.

REASON FOR REFERRAL:_____
_____
_____

INTERAGENCY REFERRAL
        FORM

Client's Name
    Address
    Phone

Referral Agency   Agency Referred to
    Address   Address
    Phone   Phone
    Referred by   Appointment with
    Date   Day of Week
                                                    Date
                                                    Time_____[ ] [ ]
                                                                a.m.   p.m.

REASON FOR REFERRAL:_____
_____
_____

INTERAGENCY REFERRAL
FORM

Client's Name
Address
Phone

Referral Agency _____   Agency Referred to _____
Address _____   Address _____
Phone _____   Phone _____
Referred by _____   Appointment with _____
Date   Day of Week _____
   Date _____
   Time _____ [ ] [ ]
   a.m. p.m.

REASON FOR REFERRAL: _____
_____
_____

INTERAGENCY REFERRAL
FORM

Client's Name
Address
Phone

Referral Agency _____   Agency Referred to _____
Address _____   Address _____
Phone _____   Phone _____
Referred by _____   Appointment with _____
Date _____   Day of Week _____
   Date _____
   Time _____ [ ] [ ]
   a.m. p.m.

REASON FOR REFERRAL: _____
_____
_____

INTERAGENCY REFERRAL
FORM

Client's Name
Address
Phone

Referral Agency _____   Agency Referred to _____
Address _____   Address _____
Phone _____   Phone _____
Referred by _____   Appointment with _____
Date _____   Day of Week _____
                                        Date _____
                                        Time _____ [ ] [ ]
                                                        a.m. p.m.

REASON FOR REFERRAL: _____
_____
_____

INTERAGENCY REFERRAL
FORM

Client's Name
Address
Phone

Referral Agency _____   Agency Referred to _____
Address _____   Address _____
Phone _____   Phone _____
Referred by _____   Appointment with _____
Date _____   Day of Week _____
                                        Date _____
                                        Time _____ [ ] [ ]
                                                        a.m. p.m.

REASON FOR REFERRAL: _____
_____
_____

INTERAGENCY REFERRAL
FORM

Client's Name
Address
Phone

Referral Agency _____   Agency Referred to _____
Address _____   Address _____
Phone _____   Phone _____
Referred by _____   Appointment with _____
Date _____   Day of Week _____
                                                       Date _____
                                                       Time _____ [ ] [ ]
                                                                     a.m. p.m.

REASON FOR REFERRAL: _____
_____
_____

INFORMATION AND REFERRAL CHECKLIST

1. Complete client information.

2. Complete referral agency information.

3. Complete the reason for referral.

4. Ask the client to wait.

5. Match the client's problem to an index listing.

6. Write all possible problem-service listings.

7. Turn to a problem-service card.

8. Determine if the service meets the client's needs.

9. If yes, write the agency name.

10. Turn to the agency card and determine client's eligibility.

11. If eligible, call the agency.

12. State your name and affiliation.

13. State the client's problem.

14. Request help from the agency.

15. Request an appointment.

16. Ask the client if the time is convenient.

17. Confirm the appointment.

18. Complete appointment information.

19. Complete helping agency information.

20. Thank the person.

21. Give the client a copy of the form.

22. Thank the client and request future contact.

23. Mail the helping agency and feedback copy.

24. File the original copy.

EPILOGUE

Congratulations! You have just completed a handbook on information and referral services. We have attempted to provide detailed descriptions of how a comprehensive information and referral system can be developed for your community. In addition, we have provided instructions in a recommended method for providing quality information and referral services. It is our sincere hope that the clients will be the ultimate beneficiaries of this experience.

APPENDIX: QUALITY CHECKS

We have included a quality check and behavioral checklist for each training lesson on how to provide information and referral services. These quality checks provide the instructor with an opportunity to observe the student's performance and evaluate whether the student has learned the skill. Each situation contained in the quality check is different from the situations already practiced by the student. Therefore, it will be a new test of the student's ability.

We recommend that the student demonstrate each skill to the instructor's satisfaction before beginning the training lesson on a new referral skill. Unsatisfactory performance should be followed by further practice, feedback, and a new quality check. In this way, you will insure that each student fully understands how to provide a referral.

Each quality check contains an introductory paragraph that can be read to the student to clarify the task. This paragraph is followed by several referral situations from which you may select. Feel free to make up new situations. For each role-playing situation, read one of the client situations to the student. Your role is to play the part of the client in need of help and/or the role of the person at the helping agency. The student is to play the part of the person providing a referral. Checklists are provided for your use in evaluating the student's performance in the referral situations.

QUALITY CHECK:
USING THE SOCIAL SERVICE DIRECTORY

To practice this skill will require a social service directory for your community. Below are several referral situations that might occur. In the following situation, assume that your agency does not offer the needed service. Use the directory to select the appropriate organization to handle the client situation. As your instructor, I will play the role of the client. (Note to instructor: Feel free to make up any additional information that is necessary.)

A 77-year-old man wants to go back to school. He dropped out of high school in the ninth grade. Now he would like to have a high school diploma, but does not know what he needs to do.

A man, who is obviously very unhappy, has been talking about committing suicide.

A young couple, with no children of their own, would like to become foster parents.

An elderly woman has been calling your agency at least three times everyday. She never seems to have a real problem, but talks for a very long time to whomever will listen. In one of the conversations with you, she confides that all she really needs is to have someone stop by her house every few days to check up on her and talk.

A man, whom you have just helped with another problem, tells you that he is having trouble getting his disabled veterans pension check. He has just moved to town in the last few months. However, since he moved he has not received a check.

CHECKLIST:
USING THE SOCIAL SERVICE DIRECTORY

1. Match the client's problem to an index listing.

2. Write all possible listings on scratch paper.

3. Turn to the problem-service card.

4. Determine if the service meets the need.

5. Determine the client's eligibility.

QUALITY CHECK:
ARRANGING AN APPOINTMENT FOR THE CLIENT

After you have used the social service directory to identify an organization that can help your client, it is important to call that agency and arrange an appointment for the client. In the following situation, assume that your agency does not offer the needed service and that you have identified an agency in the social service directory that offers the needed service. As your instructor, I will play the role of the person at the helping agency. (Note to instructor: Feel free to make up any additional information that is necessary. Each situation contains the name of an agency for the helper to call. You can have the student schedule an appointment with this agency or with an agency identified in your social service directory.)

A 77-year-old man wants to go back to school. He dropped out of high school in the ninth grade. Now he would like to have a high school diploma, but does not know what he needs to do. (You might call Continuing Education for this problem.)

A man, who is obviously very unhappy, has been talking about committing suicide. (You might call The Crisis Center for help.)

A young couple with no children of their own would like to become foster parents. (You might call The Family Court for this service.)

An elderly woman has been calling your agency at least three times everyday. She never seems to have a real problem, but talks for a very long time to whomever will listen. In one of the conversations with you, she confides that all she really needs is to have someone stop by her house every few days to check up on her and talk. (You might call Helping Hand for this service.)

A man, whom you have just helped with another problem, tells you he is having trouble getting his disabled veterans pension checks. He has just moved to town in the last few months. However, since he moved he has not received a check. (You might call the Veterans Administration for help.)

CHECKLIST:
ARRANGING AN APPOINTMENT FOR A CLIENT

1. Call the agency.
2. State name and affiliation.
3. State the client's problem.
4. Request help from the agency.
5. Request an appointment.
6. Ask the client if the appointment time is convenient.
7. Thank the person.

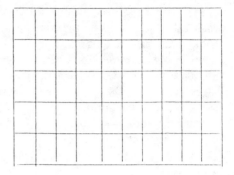

QUALITY CHECK:
COMPLETING AN INTERAGENCY REFERRAL FORM

In the following situation, assume that you have used the social service directory to locate an agency that can help your client and that you have called the helping agency and scheduled an appointment. Please complete an interagency referral form for the client situation. You may use the interagency referral forms currently used by your own agency or the forms included in this section. As your instructor, I will play the role of the client. (Note to instructor: Feel free to make up any additional information that is necessary.)

A 77-year-old man wants to go back to school to get his high school diploma. You have arranged a referral for him.

A man, who is obviously very unhappy, has been talking about committing suicide. You have scheduled an appointment with someone who can help.

You have arranged a referral for a young couple who would like to become foster parents.

You have scheduled a referral appointment for an elderly woman who needs to have someone stop by her house every few days to check up on her and talk.

You have scheduled an appointment for a man to help him get his disabled veterans pension checks now that he has moved.

INTERAGENCY REFERRAL
FORM

Client's Name
    Address
      Phone

Referral Agency_____	Agency Referred to_____
Address_____	Address_____
Phone_____	Phone_____
Referred by_____	Appointment with_____
Date_____	Day of Week_____
	Date_____
	Time_____ [ ] [ ]
	a.m. p.m.

REASON FOR REFERRAL:_____
_____
_____

INTERAGENCY REFERRAL
FORM

Client's Name
    Address
      Phone

Referral Agency_____	Agency Referred to_____
Address_____	Address_____
Phone_____	Phone_____
Referred by_____	Appointment with_____
Date_____	Day of Week_____
	Date_____
	Time_____ [ ] [ ]
	a.m. p.m.

REASON FOR REFERRAL:_____
_____
_____

INTERAGENCY REFERRAL
            FORM

Client's Name
        Address
        Phone _____ _____ ____

Referral Agency _____ __   Agency Referred to _____
        Address _____   Address _____
        Phone _____ _____   Phone _____
        Referred by _____ _____   Appointment with _____
        Date __ _____ ____   Day of Week ____ ___ ___
                                                    Date _____
                                                    Time _____[ ] [ ]
                                                          a.m. p.m.

REASON FOR REFERRAL: _____ ____
_____
_____

INTERAGENCY REFERRAL
            FORM

Client's Name
        Address
        Phone ___ ____ _____ ___

Referral Agency _____ __   Agency Referred to ____ _____ __
        Address _____   Address __ _____
        Phone _____ _____   Phone _____
        Referred by _____ _____   Appointment with _____
        Date __ _____ __ ___   Day of Week _____
                                                    Date _____
                                                    Time _____[ ] [ ]
                                                          a.m. p.m.

REASON FOR REFERRAL: _____ ___
_____
_____

INTERAGENCY REFERRAL
              FORM

Client's Name
        Address
        Phone

Referral Agency_____   Agency Referred to_____
        Address_____   Address_____
          Phone_____   Phone_____
    Referred by_____   Appointment with_____
           Date_____   Day of Week_____
                                                 Date_____
                                                 Time_____ [ ] [ ]
                                                           a.m. p.m.

REASON FOR REFERRAL:_____
_____
_____

CHECKLIST:
COMPLETING AN INTERAGENCY REFERRAL FORM

1. Complete the client information.

2. Complete the referral
agency information.

3. Complete the helping
agency information.

4. Complete the appoint-
ment information.

5. Complete the reason for
referral.

6. Give the client a copy of
the interagency referral
form.

7. Thank the client and request future contact.

8. Send the helping agency
copy and the feedback
copy to the helping
agency.

9. File the original copy.

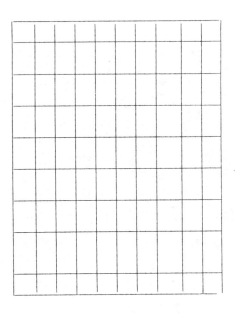

QUALITY CHECK: PROVIDING A REFERRAL

This is the final quality check. Now that you have completed
training, we have provided one last opportunity to practice all of the
skills involved in providing a referral. In the following situations
please use the social service directory to identify the appropriate
agency to handle the problem, arrange an appointment for the client,
and complete an interagency referral form. As your instructor, I will
play the role of the client and the role of the person at the helping
agency. After you have satisfactorily completed this quality check,
you will be ready to provide referrals to your real clients.

The police have come to you for help. The officer picked up a young
man, with no identification, in the park. The young man does not
appear to be on drugs; however, he is somewhat incoherent. He has not
broken any law, but the police think that he needs some help.

A woman has received a utility cut-off notice from the gas company. She does not have the money to pay the bill and is afraid that her baby will freeze.

A young boy comes in with a black eye and a split lip. He tells you that his parents are temporarily out of town and that he is staying with his uncle. It was his uncle that beat him up and he is afraid to go home.

A family comes to your agency the morning after a fire. They have lost all of their belongings in the blaze, have no insurance, and have no place to spend the night.

A woman comes to you because she is pregnant and cannot afford to pay a doctor for a prenatal check-up.

INTERAGENCY REFERRAL
FORM

Client's Name
Address
Phone

Referral Agency_____   Agency Referred to_____
Address_____   Address_____
Phone_____   Phone_____
Referred by_____   Appointment with_____
Date_____   Day of Week_____
                           Date_____
                           Time_____ [ ] [ ]
                                        a.m. p.m.

REASON FOR REFERRAL:_____

INTERAGENCY REFERRAL
FORM

Client's Name
Address
Phone

Referral Agency_____   Agency Referred to_____
Address_____   Address_____
Phone_____   Phone_____
Referred by_____   Appointment with_____
Date_____   Day of Week_____
                           Date_____
                           Time_____ [ ] [ ]
                                        a.m. p.m.

REASON FOR REFERRAL:_____

INTERAGENCY REFERRAL
        FORM

Client's Name
     Address
     Phone

Referral Agency _____   Agency Referred to _____
     Address_____   Address _____
     Phone_____   Phone _____
     Referred by_____   Appointment with _____
     Date _____   Day of Week _____
                                         Date _____
                                         Time_____ [ ] [ ]
                                                          a.m. p.m.

REASON FOR REFERRAL: _____
_____
_____

INTERAGENCY REFERRAL
        FORM

Client's Name
     Address
     Phone

Referral Agency _____   Agency Referred to _____
     Address_____   Address _____
     Phone_____   Phone _____
     Referred by_____   Appointment with _____
     Date _____   Day of Week _____
                                         Date _____
                                         Time_____ [ ] [ ]
                                                          a.m. p.m.

REASON FOR REFERRAL: _____
_____
_____

INTERAGENCY REFERRAL
FORM

Client's Name
Address
Phone

Referral Agency _____   Agency Referred to _____
Address _____   Address _____
Phone _____   Phone _____
Referred by _____   Appointment with _____
Date _____   Day of Week _____
                                                            Date _____
                                                            Time _____ [ ] [ ]
                                                                              a.m. p.m.

REASON FOR REFERRAL: _____

_____

_____

INFORMATION AND REFERRAL CHECKLIST

1. Complete client information.
2. Complete referral agency information.
3. Complete the reason for referral.
4. Ask the client to wait.
5. Match the client's problem to an index listing.
6. Write all possible problem-service listings.
7. Turn to a problem-service card.
8. Determine if the service meets the client's needs.
9. If yes, write the agency name.

10. Turn to the agency card and determine client's eligibility.

11. If eligible, call the agency.

12. State your name and affiliation.

13. State the client's problem.

14. Request help from the agency.

15. Request an appointment.

16. Ask the client if the time is convenient.

17. Confirm the appointment.

18. Complete appointment information.

19. Complete helping agency information.

20. Thank the person.

21. Give the client a copy of the form.

22. Thank the client and request future contact.

23. Mail the helping agency and feedback copy.

24. File the original copy.

REFERENCES

D'AUGELLI, A.R., DANISH, S.J., and BROCK, G.W. Untrained paraprofessionals' verbal helping behavior: Description and implications for training. *American Journal of Community Psychology,* 1976, *4,* 275-283.

FAWCETT, S.B., FLETCHER, R.K., and MATHEWS, R.M. Applications of behavior analysis in community education. In D. Glenwick and L. Jason (Eds.), *Behavioral community psychology: Progress and prospects.* New York: Praeger, 1980.

FREIRE, P. *Pedagogy of the oppressed.* New York: Herder & Herder, 1970.

HALLOWITZ, E., and RIESSMAN, F. The role of the indigenous nonprofessional in a community mental health neighborhood service center. *American Journal of Orthopsychiatry,* 1967, *37,* 766-778.

MATHEWS, R.M., and FAWCETT, S.B. Assessing dissemination capability: An evaluation of an exportable training package. *Behavior Modification,* 1979, *3,* 49-62. (a)

MATHEWS, R.M., and FAWCETT, S.B. Community information systems: Analysis of an agency referral program. *Journal of Community Psychology,* 1979, *7,* 281-289. (b)

MATHEWS, R.M., and FAWCETT, S.B. A community-based information and referral system. *Journal of the Community Development Society,* 1979, *10,* 13-25. (c)

ABOUT THE AUTHORS

R. MARK MATHEWS (Ph.D., University of Kansas, 1980) is currently Assistant Professor of Psychology at the University of Hawaii at Hilo. His major research interests include the development and analysis of community service programs, the evaluation of educational interventions, and the assessment and training of job-finding skills. Dr. Mathews serves as a consulting editor for such journals as the *American Journal of Community Psychology, Behavioral Assessment, Behavior Therapy,* and *Journal of Applied Behavior Analysis.*

STEPHEN B. FAWCETT (Ph.D., University of Kansas, 1974) is Associate Professor of Human Development and Coordinator of the Community Development Program at the Center for Public Affairs at the University of Kansas. Dr. Fawcett is author of numerous articles and book chapters on the subjects of community service delivery, competency-based instruction, and community development. He is on the Board of Editors or a consulting editor for such journals as *American Journal of Community Psychology, Journal of Applied Behavior Analysis, Journal of Personalized Instruction, Behavioral Assessment,* and *Policy Studies Journal.* He is coauthor of the forthcoming books *Learning Counseling and Problem-solving Skills* and *Optimizing and Evaluating Public Policy.*